JAZZ SCALES for BASS

by COREY CHRISTIANSEN and JAY FARMER

Online Audio www.melbay.com/99778BCDEB

ONLINE CONTENTS

I0806900

2 3 4 5 6 7 8 9 0

Visit us on the Web at www.melbay.com — E-mail us at email@melbay.com

Contents

Introduction

This book will give bassists insight into many of the scales used in jazz. While techniques and ideas of the jazz language outside of scales are not specifically addressed in this book, it is hoped the student will learn where and how different scales may be applied in jazz improvisation. Each scale will be presented with standard notation, tablature, and fingering patterns. Recordings of the chord progressions and etudes have been provided so the student can hear how these scales may be used in real life situations.

There is no alternative for listening to great jazz recordings. Find jazz recordings where the scales in discussion have been used to create great music. It will be easier for the student to apply these scales and sounds into their playing if they have been inspired by hearing master musicians doing the same.

Practice each of these scales slowly until it is flawless in sound quality, dynamics, and time. Too often, students practice fast and sloppy. If you can play something slow and perfect, it will be easier to play it fast. Work on perfection before working on speed. As a gunslinger in the Old West, it would have been unwise to work only on speed and not accuracy. So it is with music; however, our lives are not on the line when we play music. There are a lot of musicians who try to play fast but lose the desired effect due to inaccuracy and a lack of control. Good luck and enjoy practicing the scales presented in this book.

Fingerings

Each new scale is accompanied by a one-octave and two-octave fingering diagram. One-octave scales can be played across the strings in one or two positions; however, a more linear approach is required to facilitate a two-octave range. As the scale moves up the fingerboard, carefully observe the linear shifts involved in the two-octave fingering patterns. A thorough knowledge of the fingerboard will undoubtedly make the series of shifts easier to grasp and commit to memory.

The scale fingerings presented are applicable for both electric and upright bass. Upright players can convert the 4-finger system to the 3-finger system by simply replacing any half step fingering of 3-4 with 2-4 and any whole step fingering of 2-4 with 1-3. The 3-finger system used in upright bass technique works well on electric bass for those players with smaller hands or for those who simply want to reduce the large stretches in the lower positions. The 3-finger system (1-2-4) uses the 3rd and 4th fingers (collectively called 4th finger) on one fret. For example, to play the notes F-F♯-G on the 4th string, first finger plays F, second finger plays F♯, and the third and fourth finger are used to play G on the third fret.

Major Scales

Major Scales

A scale is an orderly succession of notes which can be sung or played on an instrument. Composers and musicians who use improvisation (spontaneous composition) in their music have used scales to create melodies and construct harmonies for centuries. As a jazz musician, it is important to have an arsenal of scales to choose from when improvising and composing.

The major scale consists of two whole steps, a half step, three more whole steps followed by another half step. In the key of C, no accidentals (sharps or flats) will be needed. The notes that make up a C major scale are C, D, E, F, G, A, B, and the octave is completed with C. Found below are the standard notation and TAB for this scale.

Construction: whole step, whole step, half step, whole step, whole step, whole step, half step

C Major

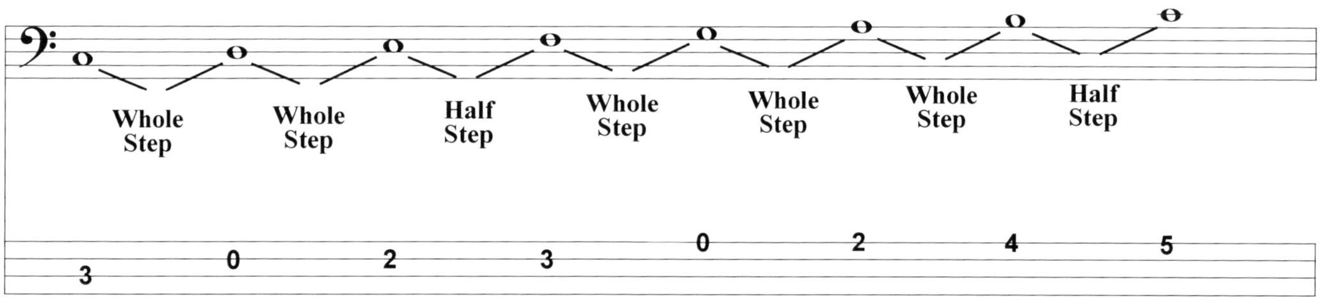

It is important to recognize where the whole steps and half steps occur in the major scale. For this purpose, an F major scale has been constructed solely on the fourth string. Because of the linear motion used in this fingering for the scale, this fingering is not the most practical pattern when improvising. However, it does show where the whole and half steps are in the scale. It is a good idea to practice the scales on each of the four strings individually. The scales in this book will be presented with finger patterns and diagrams along with the scale constructed on only one string. It is the responsibility of the student to figure out and practice all scales in a linear fashion on each of the four strings.

F Major

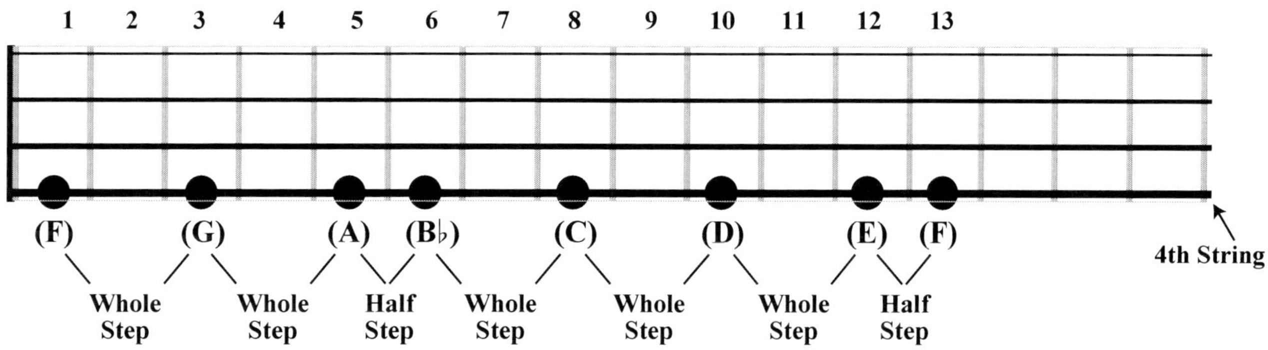

Having a systemized approach to practicing scales in all twelve keys is very important. It is suggested that the major scales presented be practiced around the circle of fourths. The keys in the circle of fourths are as follows: C, F, B♭, E♭, A♭, D♭, G♭, B, E, A, D, G, and back to C. This circle is created by starting with a C major scale and locating the fourth degree, which is F, by playing up the scales first four notes (C, D, E, and F). To find the next key which is fourth away from F, simply play up the F major scale four notes. This will result in a B♭ being played. This pattern should be followed back to the original key of C to find all of the major keys. A chart has been provided which shows the circle of fourths and how the first few keys in the circle are derived. All twelve keys will be covered by practicing the major scale around the circle of fourths. This activity should be repeated for all scales learned in the future.

Circle of Fourths

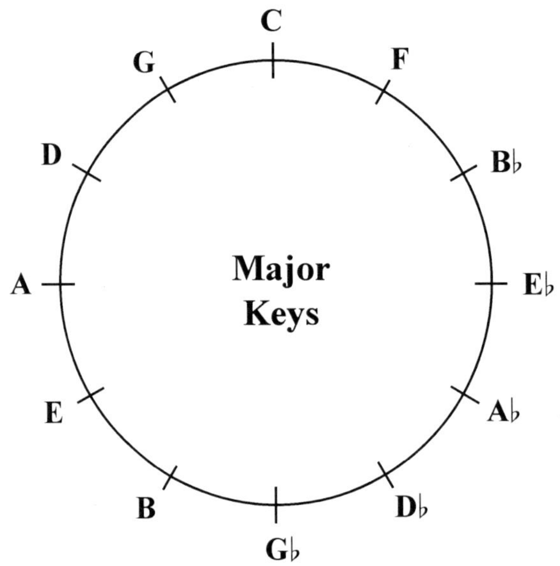

C Major Scale

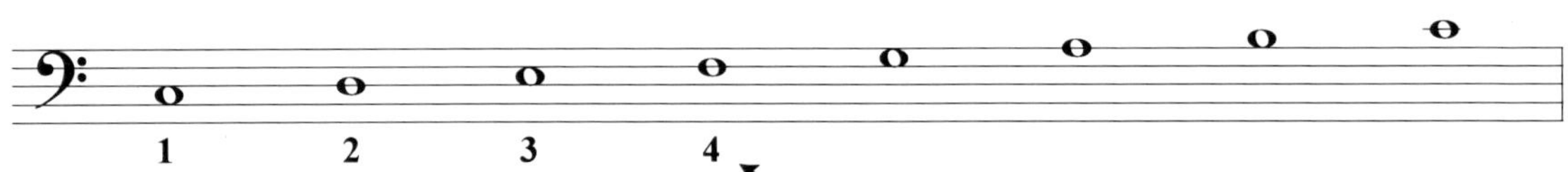

F becomes the root for next major scale.

F Major Scale

B♭ becomes the root for next major scale.

B♭ Major Scale

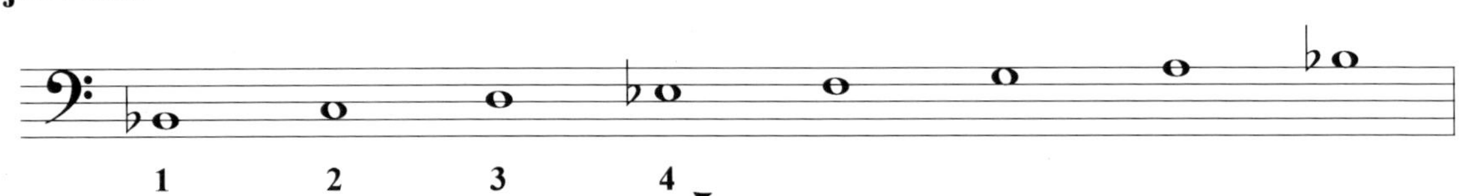

E♭ becomes the root for next major scale and so on back to CMajor.

The circle of fourths sequence remains the same regardless of what scale is being practiced. The circle is based on the interval of a perfect fourth which is found in the major scale. Some scales in this book may have altered fourth degree; however, do not change the practice sequence based on these alterations.

One exercise that will help any bassist memorize and master scales is practicing scales on octave at a time. Use the following charts and fingering patterns to master scales in all twelve keys.

These charts show the natural notes on each string of the bass.

Remember, to flat (♭) a note, move down one fret (one half step). To sharp (♯) a note, move up one fret (one half step).

Root Notes on the E String

0	1	3	5	7	8	10	12
E	F	G	A	B	C	D	E

Root Notes on the A String

0	2	3	5	7	8	10	12
A	B	C	D	E	F	G	A

Root Notes on the D String

0	2	3	5	7	9	10	12
D	E	F	G	A	B	C	D

Root Notes on the G String

0	2	4	5	7	9	10	12
G	A	B	C	D	E	F	G

One-Octave Major Scale

◆ = **Root Notes**

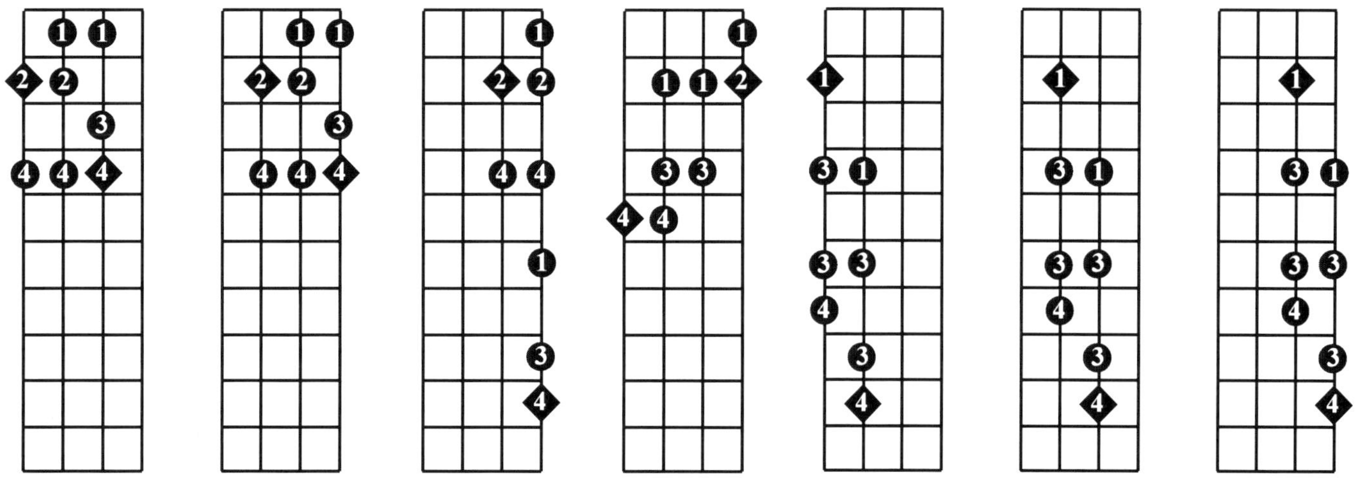

When one-octave scales have been mastered, the bassist can practice two-octave major scales. Moveable finger patterns for the two-octave major scale are shown below. Practice these fingerings in all twelve keys.

Two-octave patterns can be created by combining two one-octave patterns. Experiment with creating new two-octave fingerings.

Two-Octave Major

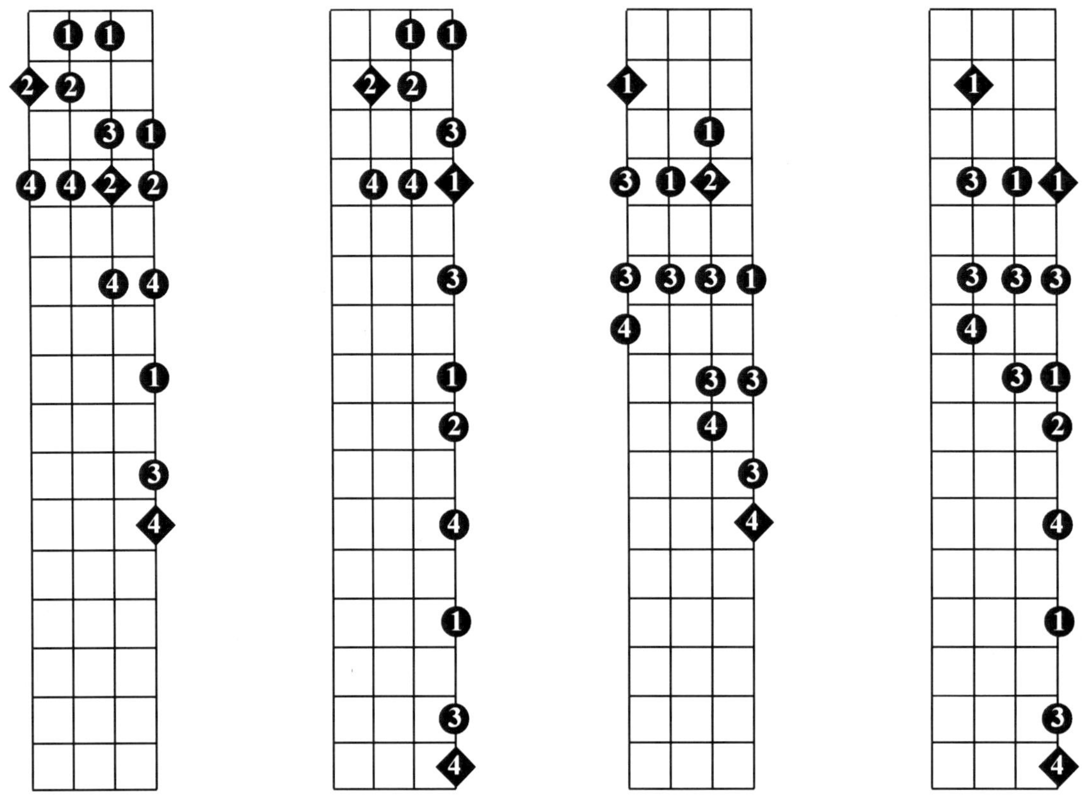

(The scale diagrams provided are only suggestions. By understanding the construction of any scale, the bassist may figure out fingerings that work best for them.)

It is common to practice scales starting on the lowest root note. Play them ascending and then descending. To increase scale familiarity, also practice the major scale in the opposite order. Start on a higher root note and play the scale descending and ascending. This exercise will help the student refrain from always starting on the lowest note in the scale and moving up when improvising. Becoming familiar with the scale in all positions and in all areas of the fretboard is important when mastering scales to be used in jazz improvisation.

Playing scalar patterns or sequenced patterns of notes through a scale is an effective way to become familiar with each of the scales. Scalar patterns build technique and help the player become proficient at playing the scale. A few of these patterns are shown for the major scale below. It is expected the student will practice these and other scalar patterns for each of the scales covered in the chapter.

Sequence #1

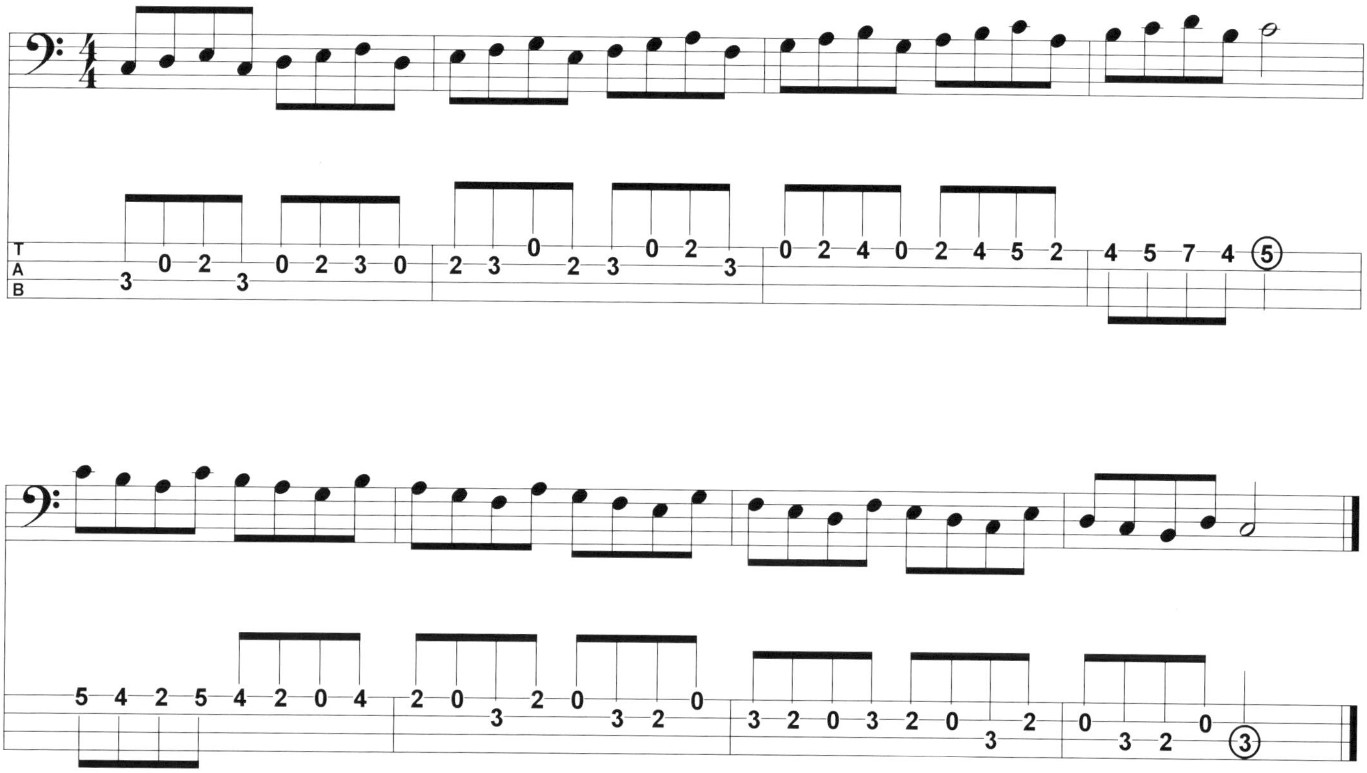

Sequence #2

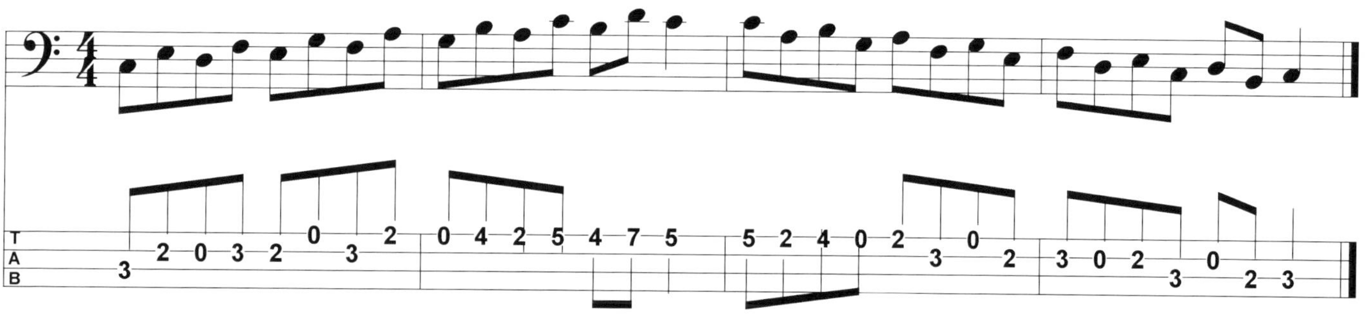

Sequence #3

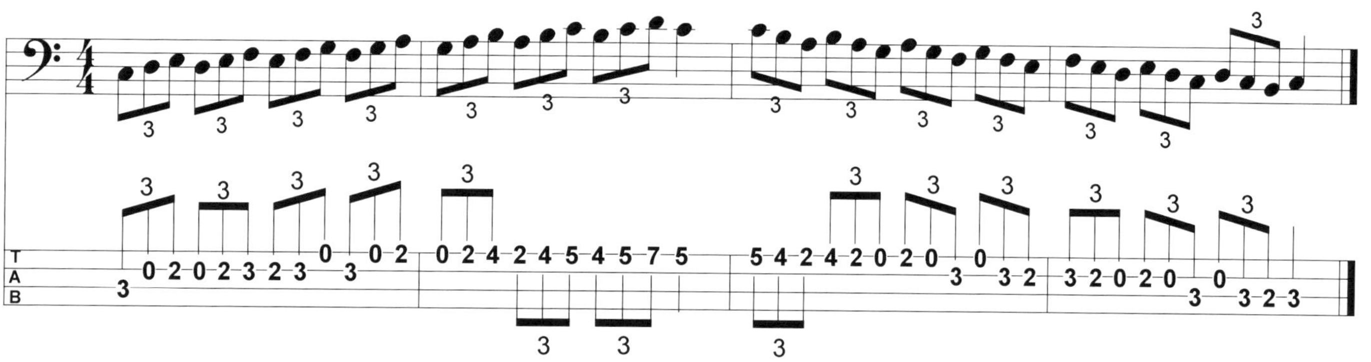

To create original scalar patterns (sequences), simply assign each of the notes in the scale a number. The chart below shows assigned numbers for each of the notes in a major scale with the root on the fourth string. Next, a numerical pattern is formulated. Start out with a simple pattern such as: 1234, 2345, 3456, and so on until all of the assigned notes are used. Simply play the notes in the order of the pattern. Practice formulating many scalar patterns. It is suggested that pattern groupings stay between two and four notes. This is a great exercise and it is expected the student will play scalar patterns for all of the scales in this book.

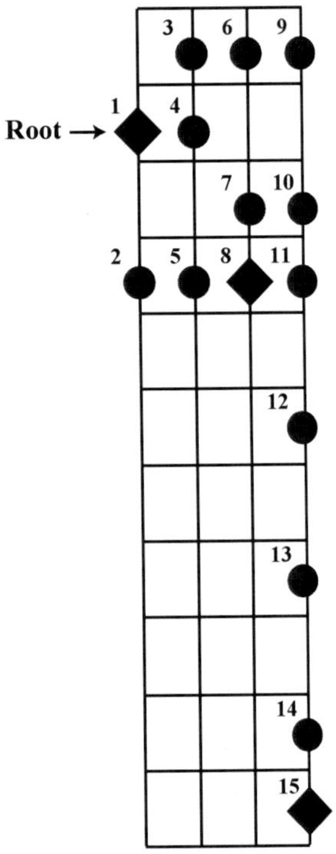

Sample Numerical Sequences:

1-2-3, 2-3-4, 3-4-5, 4-5-6, etc.

1-3, 2-4, 3-5, 4-6, 5-7, etc.

8-6, 7-5, 6-4, 5-3, etc.

8-7-6, 7-6-5, 6-5-4, 5-4-3, etc.

Practice playing the major scale against the following rhythm track vamps found on the companion audio. The vamp changes key every eight measures (four bars repeated). Because the chords are modulating around the circle of fourths, the major scales being practiced should move with the chords. The major scale being practiced should coincide with the major chord. Each scale should be mastered in ascending and descending form, as well as with sequences or scalar patterns. Later, when this scale has been mastered, it will seem easier to improvise and create melodies with this scale.

For all the rhythm tracks in this text, play the scale that corresponds to the letter name of the chord being played. (For example, play a C major scale for a CMaj7 chord, play a G major scale for a GMaj7 chord, play B-flat Mixolydian mode for a B♭7 chord, etc.)

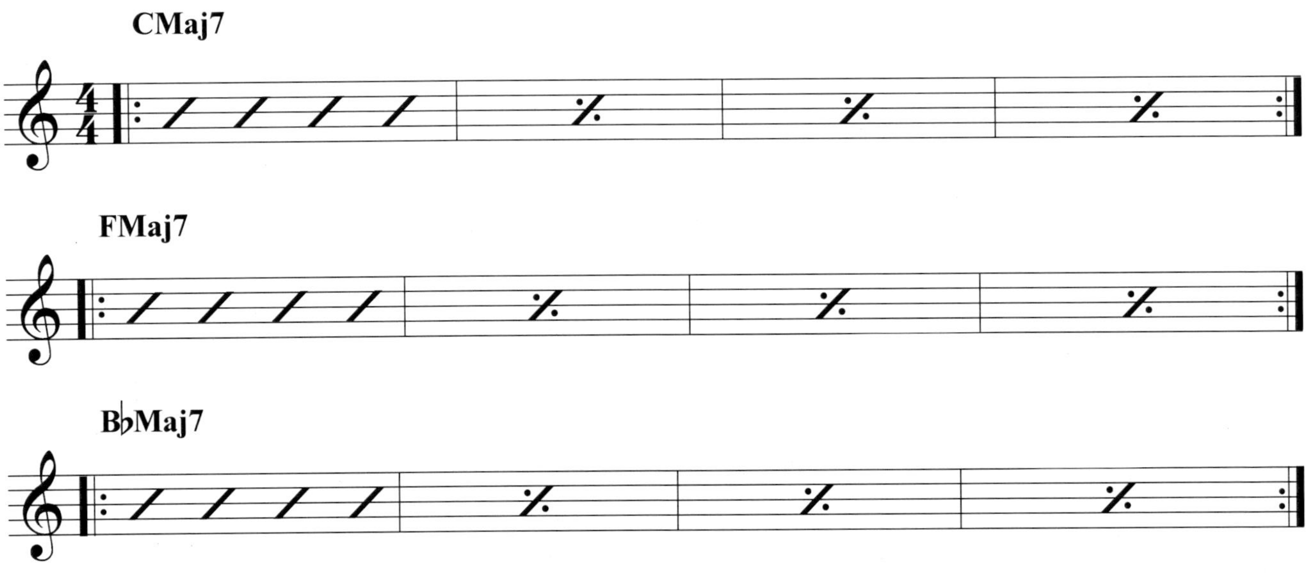

The major scale may be used to improvise and create melodies against the major chord that has the same letter name as the scale. The major scale may be used against any of the basic embellishments of a major chord which include: 6th, maj7, maj9, add 9, 6/9, maj13, and all of these when they contain a suspended fourth (sus or sus 4). The major scale may be used against any of the chords (and their respective embellishments) derived from the same major scale. In the key of C this would include: C major, D minor, E minor, G major, G major (the five chord in a major key can be a dominant seventh, G7), A minor, and B diminished. It is hoped that eventually the student will be able to "play the changes." (Play notes, lines, and scalar ideas that bring out the differences in chords rather than the similarities.) Being able to recognize the scale by which a group of chords have been born will be a great asset to any player.

Practice the following exercise which makes use of the G major scale.

CD #3

Because the written etudes for each scale are eight measures long and are written over a one chord vamp, they may be transposed and played over all twelve keys supplied by the rhythm vamp. While transposing may be challenging at first to the student, this practice will insure mastery of the scales presented in this book.

An interval is the distance between two notes. The following chart shows the whole step and half step relationship for all of the intervals found in the scales presented in this book. The major scale's construction yields all the "major" and "perfect" intervals that correspond directly to how many notes in the scale they are away from the tonic (note that names of the scale). For example, in the key of C major, D is a major second interval (D is the second note in the scale), E is a major third (E is the third note in the scale), F is a perfect fourth (F is the fourth note in the scale), G is a perfect fifth (G is the fifth note in the scale), A is a major sixth (A is the sixth note in the scale), and B is a major seventh (B is the seventh note in the scale. Every scale is built upon the concept of intervals.

When an interval or scale degree is referred to as lowered, it means that the note is lowered by one half step (one fret on guitar). When an interval is referred to as raised, it means that the note is raised by one half step. A minor interval is a major interval that has been lowered by one half step. An augmented interval is a major or perfect interval (the term perfect interval is only used for the intervals of a fourth, fifth, and octave) that has been raised by one half step. A diminished interval is a perfect interval that has been lowered by one half step.

Interval	Symbol	Number of Steps from Root
Tonic	Root (1)	
Minor Second	m2	One Half Step
Major Second	M2	One Whole Step
Augmented Second	A2	One and a Half Steps
Minor Third	m3	One and a Half Steps
Major Third	M3	Two Whole Steps
Augmented Third	A3	Two and a Half Steps
Diminished Fourth	D4	Two Whole Steps
Perfect Fourth	P4	Two and a Half Steps
Augmented Fourth	A4	Three Whole Steps
Diminished Fifth	D5	Three Whole Steps
Perfect Fifth	P5	Three and a Half Steps
Augmented Fifth	A5	Four Whole Steps
Minor Sixth	m6	Four Whole Steps
Major Sixth	M6	Four and a Half Steps
Augmented Sixth	A6	Five Whole Steps
Minor Seventh	m7	Five Whole Steps
Major Seventh	M7	Five and a Half Steps

Intervals with a number higher than a seventh have the same note name as the lower numbered interval given in parentheses. The higher number suggests that the note is played an octave higher.

Minor Ninth	m9 (m2)	Six and a Half Steps
Major Ninth	M9 (M2)	Seven Whole Steps
Augmented Ninth	A9 (A2)	Seven and a Half Steps
Diminished Eleventh	D11 (D4)	Eight Whole Steps
Perfect Eleventh	P11 (P4)	Eight and a Half Steps
Augmented Eleventh	A11 (A4)	Nine Whole Steps
Minor Thirteenth	m13 (m6)	Ten Whole Steps
Major Thirteenth	M13 (M6)	Ten and a Half Steps

Major Scale Modes

There are six other scales contained within the major scale. These other scales are called modes. Each of these modes use one of the notes from the major scale as their root note. The other notes remain the same as they were in the major scale and are played in the same alphabetical order to complete an octave. The names of the modes are: Dorian, Phrygian, Lydian, Mixolydian, Aeolian, and Locrian. Ionian is the modal name for the major scale. The following chart shows each of the modes derived from a C major scale.

Notes in C Major	Mode Derived
C	Ionian
D	Dorian
E	Phrygian
F	Lydian
G	Mixolydian
A	Aeolian
B	Locrian

Aeolian Mode

The first mode to be discussed is the Aeolian mode. It is also referred to as the natural minor scale. The root note of this mode is the sixth step of a major scale. As shown in the chart above, the A Aeolian mode (natural minor scale) has the same notes as a C major scale. The root note for this mode is the sixth note in any major scale. For example, the G major scale contains all of the notes for the E Aeolian mode. The Aeolian mode is also known as the relative minor of a major scale.

C Major

Root note for A Aeolian mode

C	D	E	F	G	A	B
1	2	3	4	5	6	7

Notes in A Aeolian mode

A B C D E F G

G Major

Root note for E Aeolian mode

G	A	B	C	D	E	F♯
1	2	3	4	5	6	7

Notes in E Aeolian mode

E F♯ G A B C D

The following charts show the construction of the Aeolian mode in whole steps and half steps, standard notation, TAB, and a linear diagram of the mode on only the fourth string with the root as an F note in the first fret. It is suggested that this mode first be played on one string only for each of the four strings. The student will become familiar with the fretboard and the relationship of whole steps and half steps which make up this mode.

Construction: whole step, half step, whole step, whole step, half step, whole step, whole step

A Aeolian (natural minor)

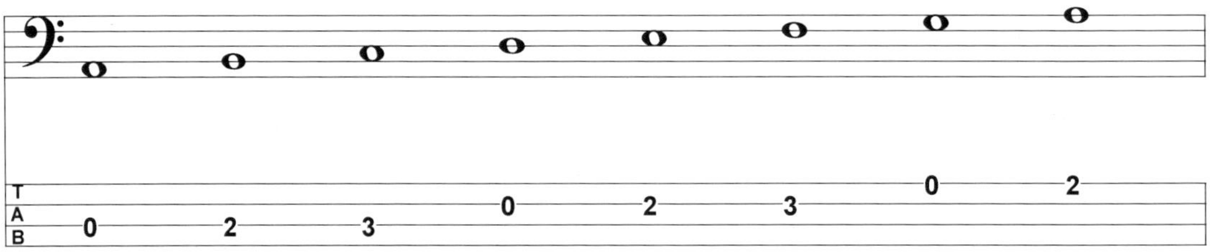

F Aeolian

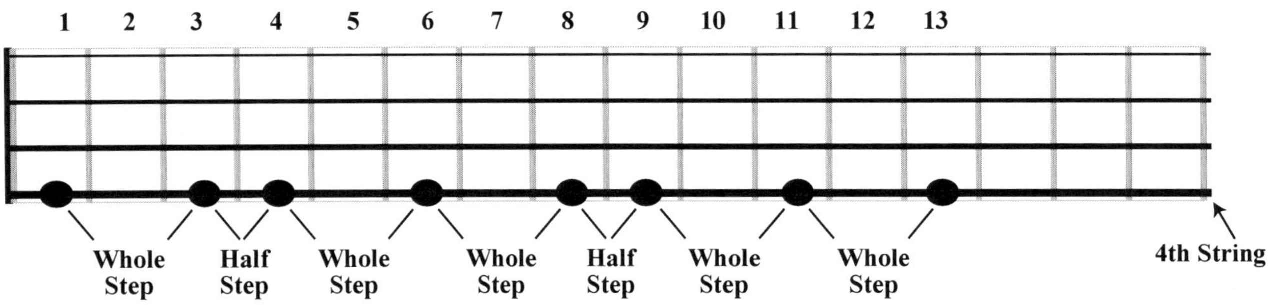

It can be seen that the A Aeolian mode or A natural minor scale contains the same notes as the C major scale. To better understand the construction of this mode (scale), it should also be related to a parallel major scale. The Aeolian mode differs from the major scale in that the third, sixth, and seventh degrees are flatted (lowered) one half step. The C major scale has no sharps or flats, whereas the C Aeolian mode contains the notes C, D, E♭, F, G, A♭, and B♭.

C major scale **C natural minor scale**

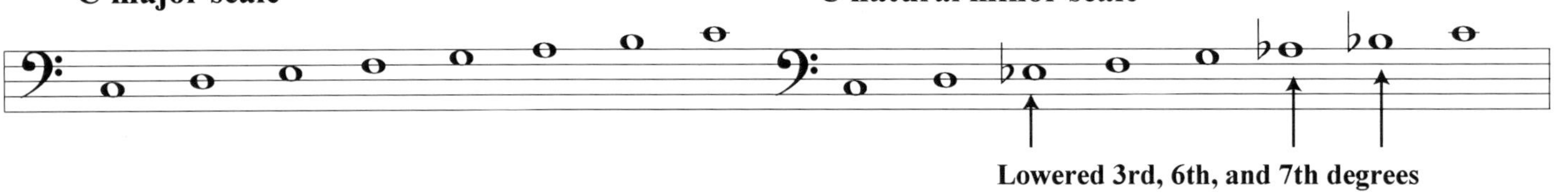

To master playing the Aeolian mode (natural minor scale), follow the same practice sequence that was given for the major scale. Play the mode/scale in one key with the root on strings four, three, and two using the different finger patterns shown below.

One-Octave Patterns - Aeolian

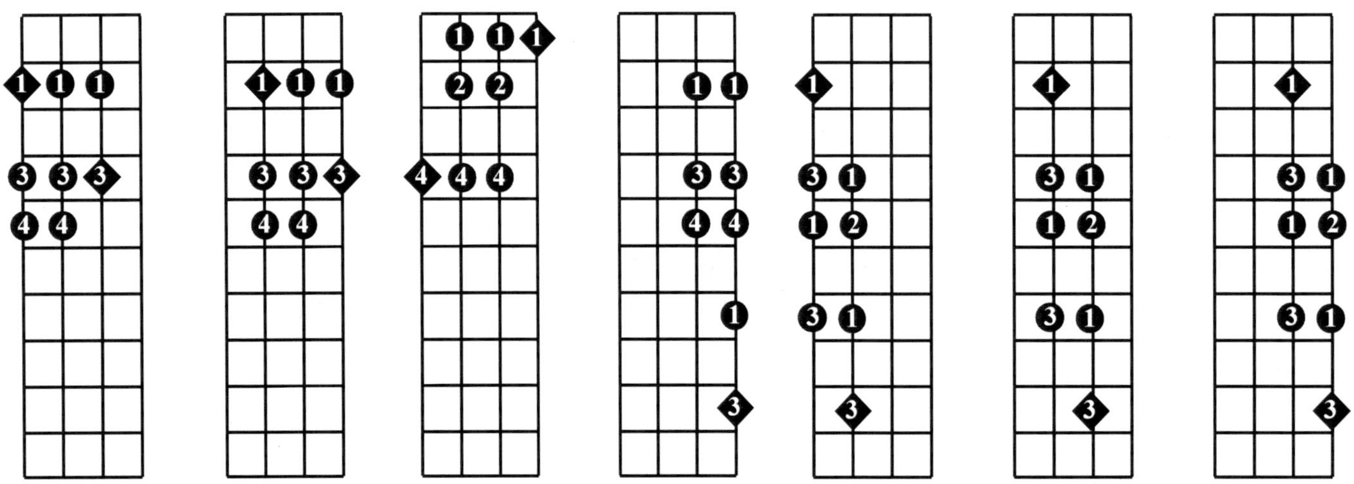

Next, each of the one-octave scales should be played in all twelve keys around the circle of fourths. After one-octave scales are played comfortably in all twelve keys, two-octave scales may be learned by using the patterns shown below.

Two-Octave Patterns - Aeolian

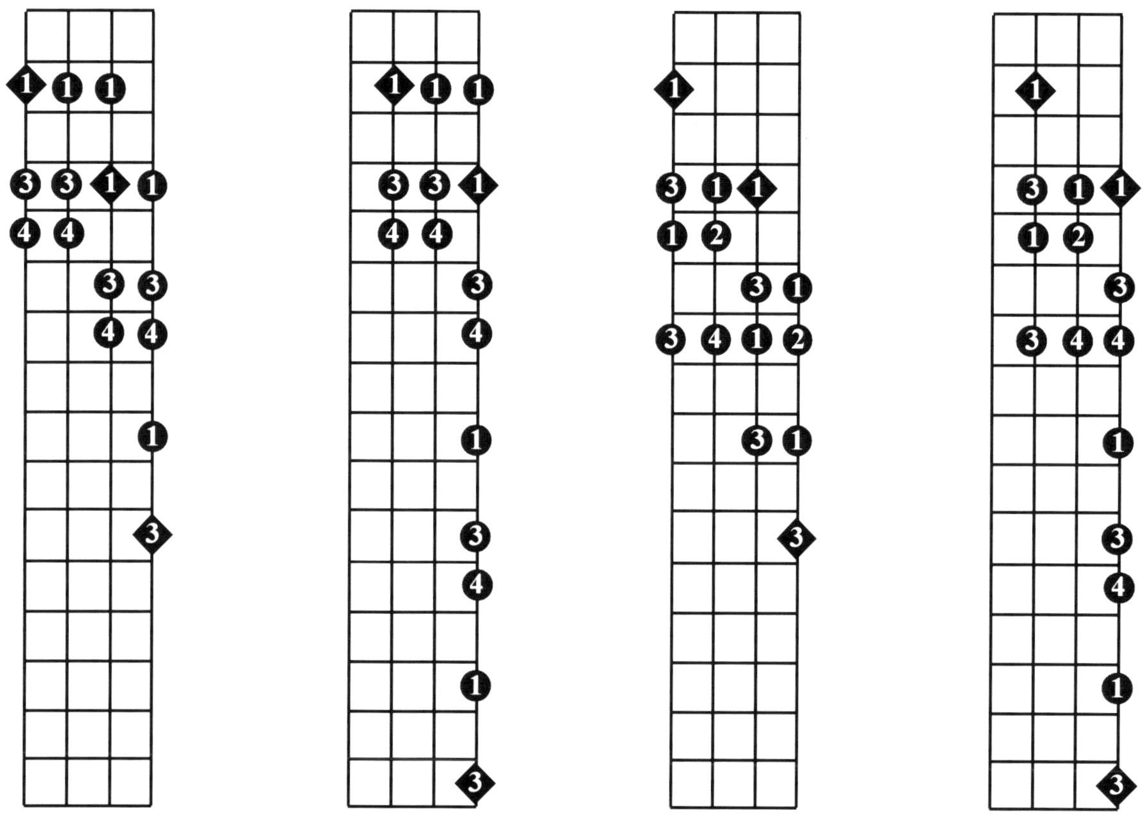

Sequencing (scalar patterns) must be played using this scale. Also, start each scale on the highest note and play it in descending and ascending fashion. Too often, bassists start on the lowest note and play the scale in ascending then descending form only.

Because the Aeolian mode is the same scale as the natural minor scale, it may be used to improvise over minor, minor seventh, minor ninth and minor suspended (m11) chords. Practice the Aeolian mode or natural minor scale using the techniques suggested above (and from the section on the major scale) over the following minor vamp. So all twelve keys will be practiced, this vamp also modulates around the circle of fourths.

CD #4

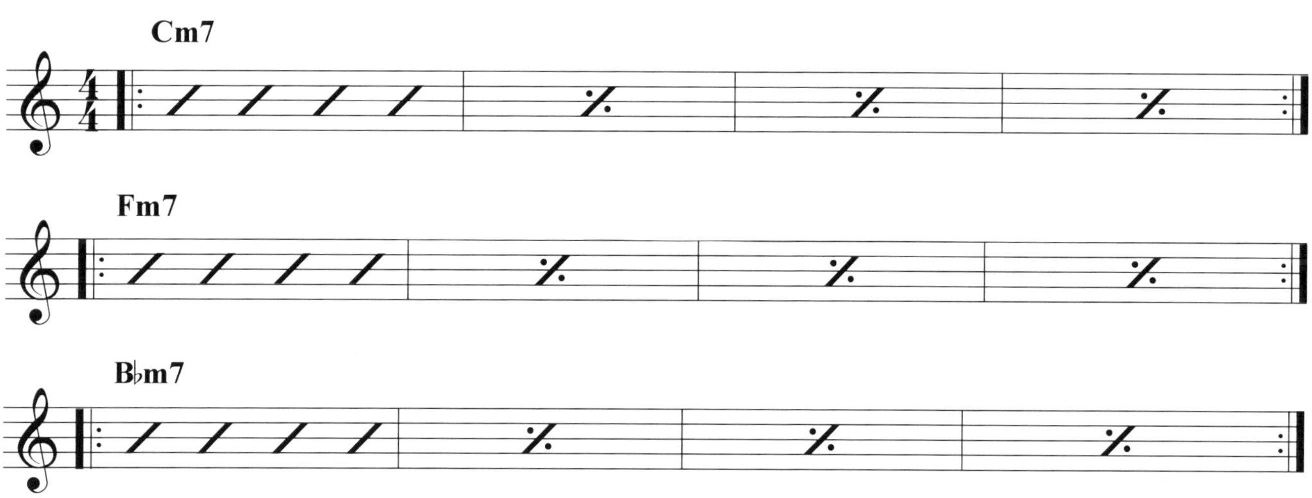

The following exercise makes use of the A Aeolian mode.

CD #5

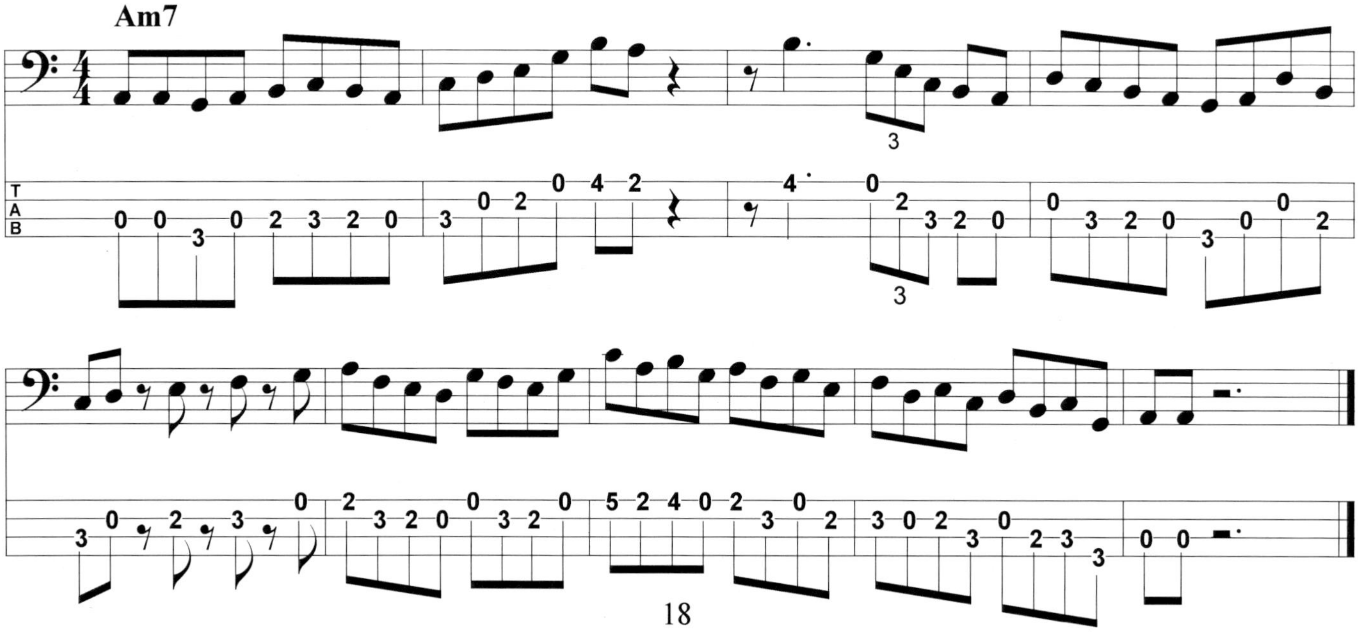

Dorian Mode

The Dorian mode starts and ends on the second degree (step) of the major scale. Therefore, the D Dorian mode makes use of the same notes as a C major scale. The Dorian mode has a minor quality and is used frequently in jazz improvisation to play over minor type chords. The Dorian mode's construction is similar to the Aeolian mode, however the sixth degree is raised (sharped) one half step.

C Major **D Dorian**

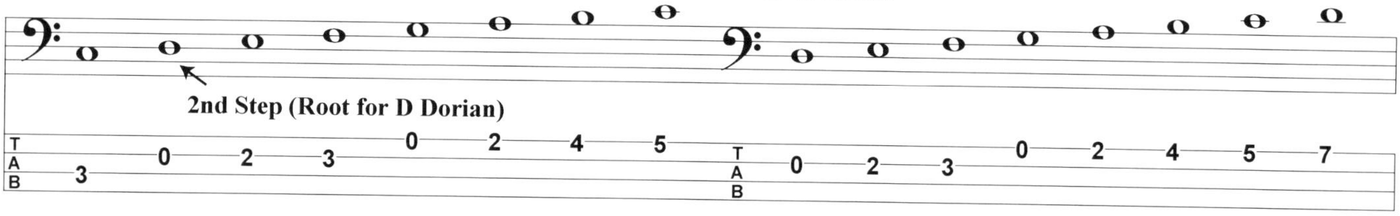

A Aeolian **A Dorian**

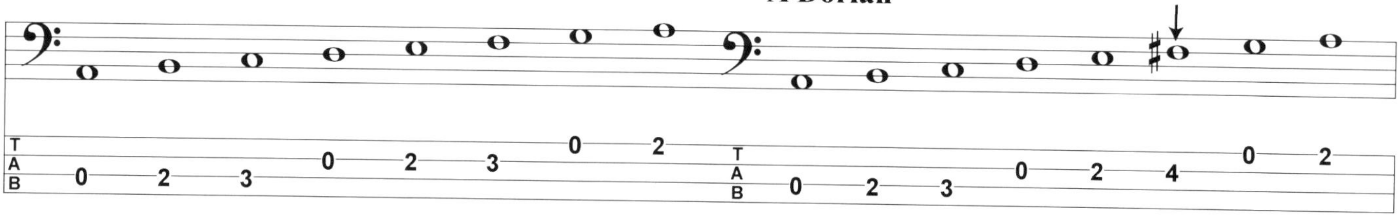

Show below is the intervallic construction of the Dorian mode. Also, the Dorian mode is shown linearly on only the fourth string with an F as the root. One-octave and two-octave patterns are also shown. Remember to practice this mode following the same routine outlined for the major scale. Because the Dorian mode has a minor quality about it, it sounds nice when played against minor sixth, minor seventh, minor ninth, minor eleventh, and minor thirteenth chords. A chord vamp has been provided so the student may practice along with harmony that moves around the circle of fourths.

Construction: whole step, half step, whole step, whole step, whole step, half step, whole step.

F Dorian

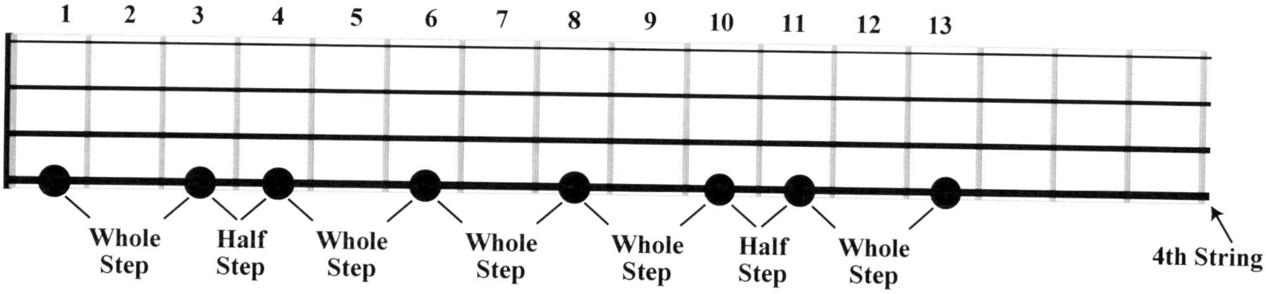

One-Octave Patterns - Dorian

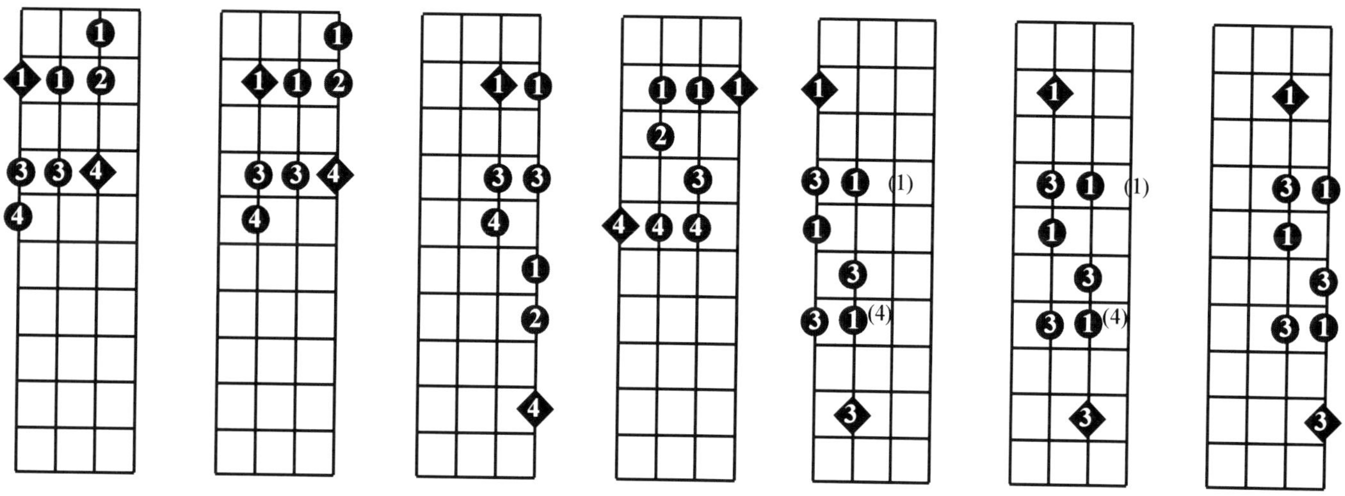

Two-Octave Patterns – Dorian

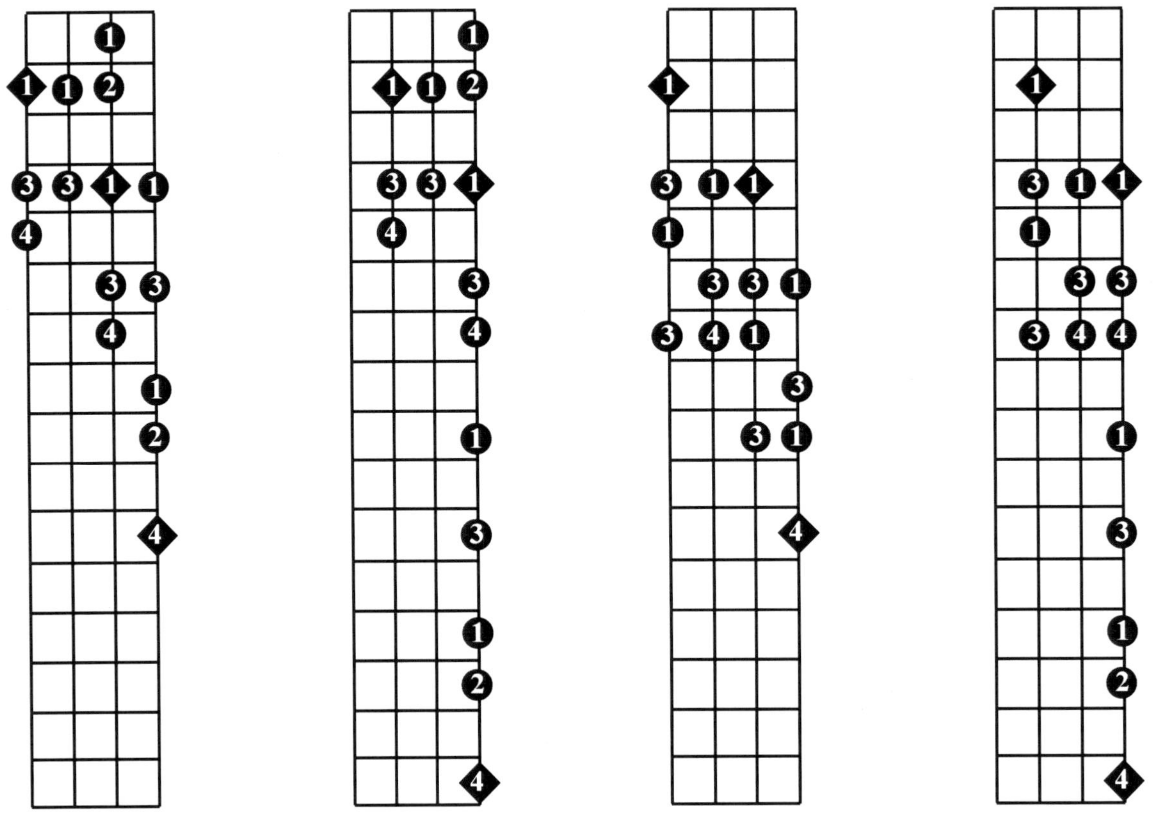

CD #4

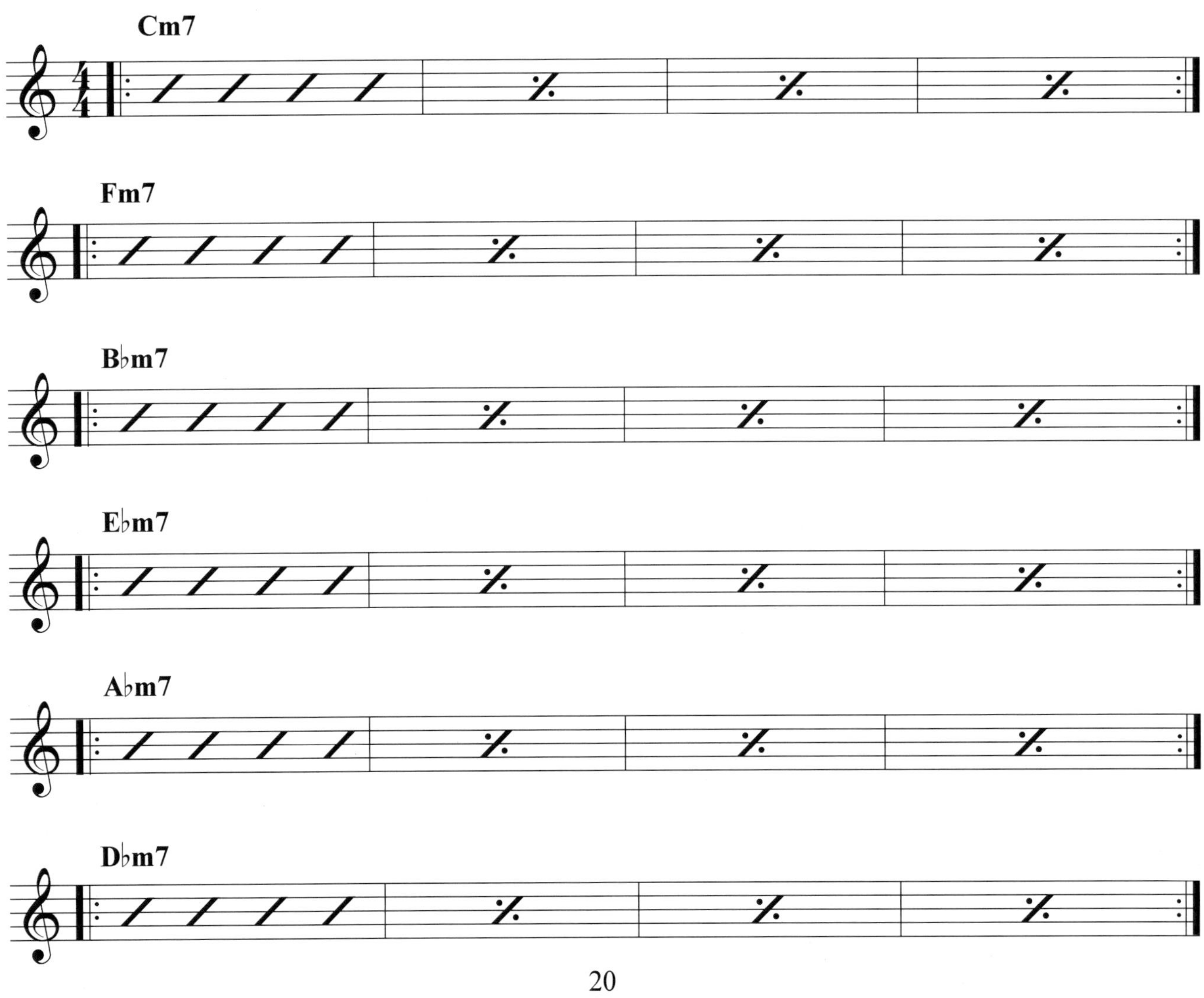

The following exercise makes use of the G Dorian mode.

CD #6

Phrygian Mode

The root of the Phrygian mode is the third step in a major scale. E Phrygian would contain the same notes as C major. (E is the third step of a C major scale.) Like the Dorian mode, the Phrygian mode has a minor quality about it. However, it differs from the minor scale (Aeolian mode) in that it has a flatted second degree. The notes contained in the A Phrygian mode are: A, B♭, C, D, E, F, and G. Notice that these are the same notes which make up an F major scale. (The note A is the third degree of an F major scale. When it is treated as the root of a mode, it will yield the Phrygian mode.)

C Major **E Phrygian**

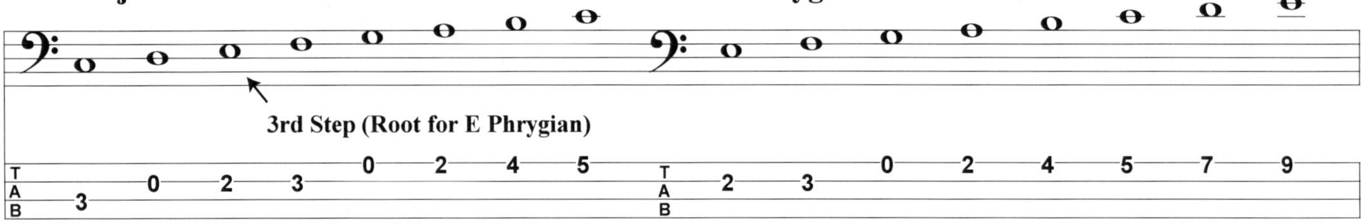

A Aeolian Mode **A Phrygian Mode**

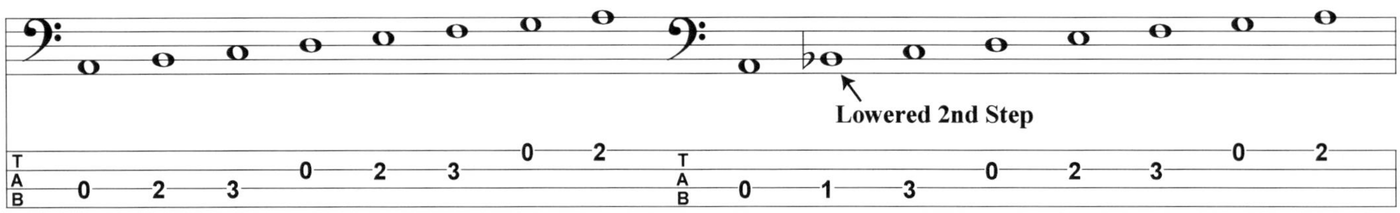

The intervallic make-up of the Phrygian mode is shown below. The linear diagram shows the Phrygian mode in the key of F. Only the sixth string is used so that whole and half steps may be seen clearly. Use the one-octave and two-octave finger patterns to learn this mode in all twelve keys. Practice this mode in descending and ascending order, as well as ascending and descending. Become completely familiar with this mode by assigning each note a number to create scalar patterns and sequences.

Construction: half step, whole step, whole step, whole step, half step, whole step, whole step.

F Phrygian

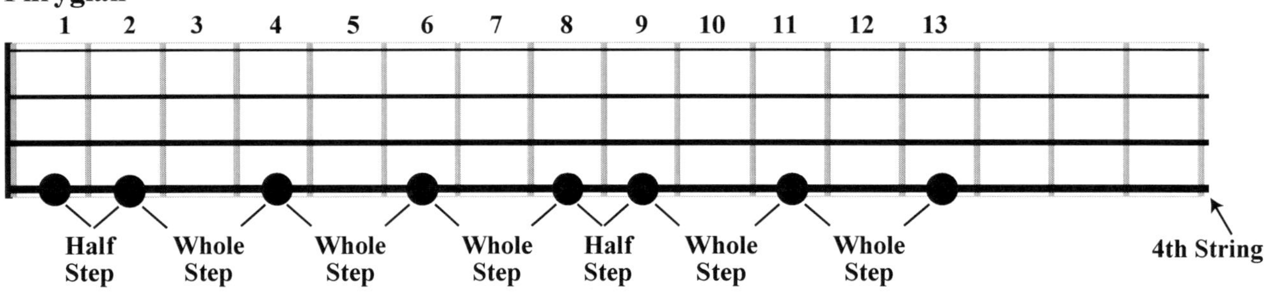

One-Octave Patterns - Phrygian

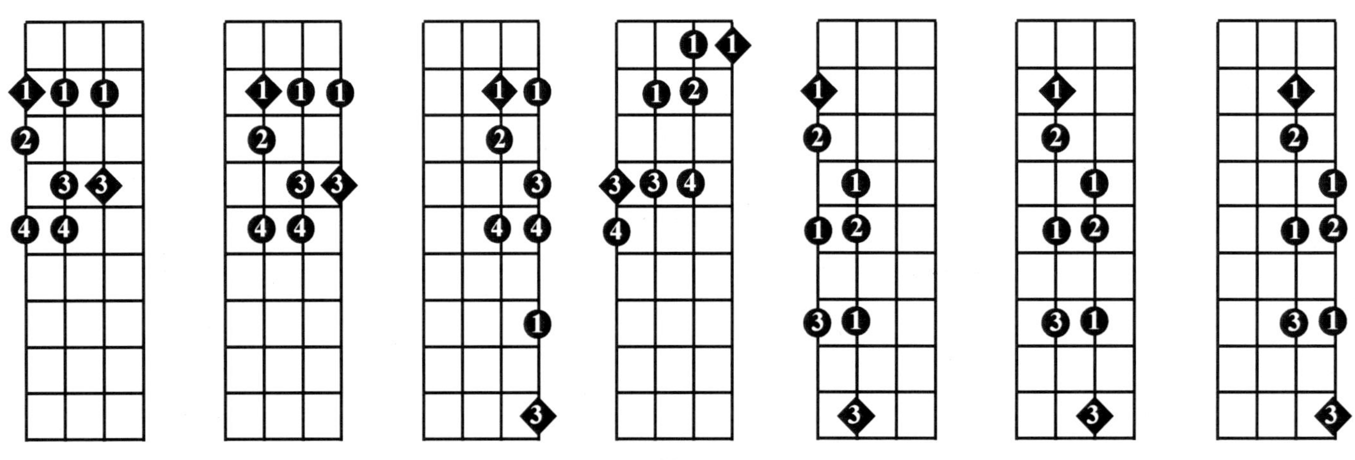

Two-Octave Patterns – Phrygian

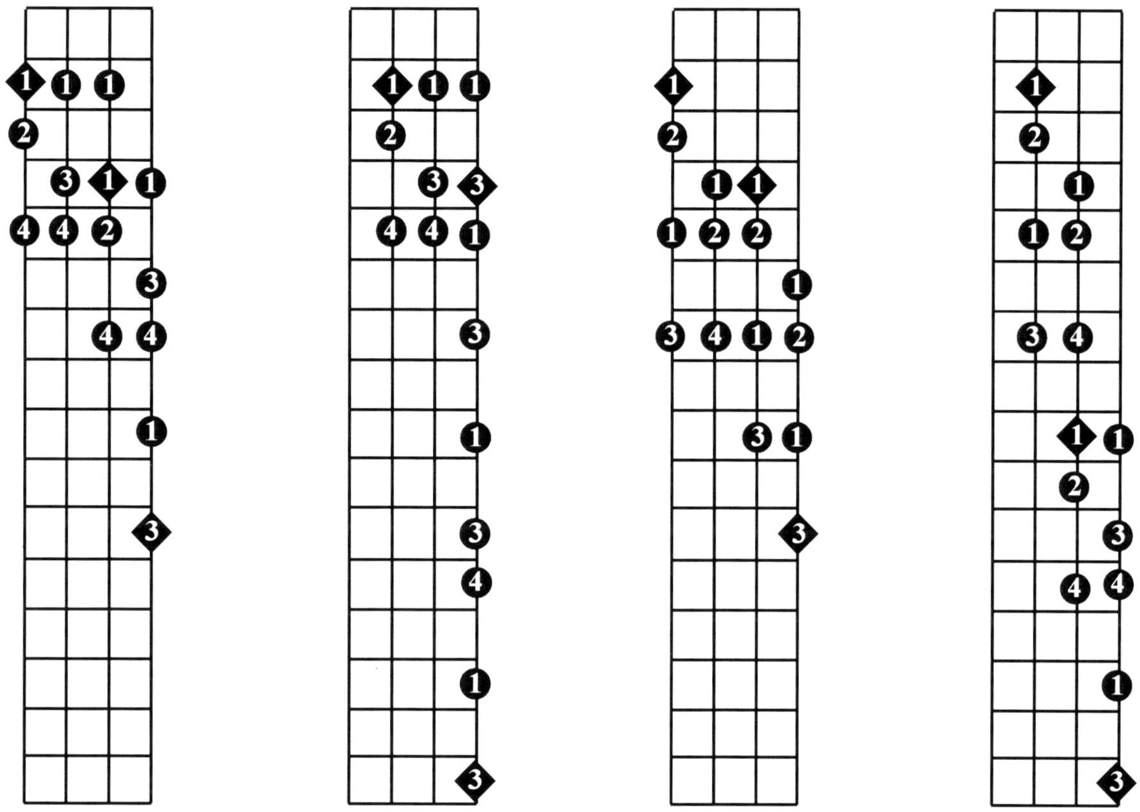

The Phrygian mode may be used to improvise against minor and minor seventh chords. However, this scale will give a "Spanish" sound if it is used against a major chord in the same key (i.e., E Phrygian mode against an E major chord). The chord vamp on the companion audio will provide a minor harmonic basis, moving in fourths to play this mode against.

CD #7 (also try with #2 for the "Spanish" sound)

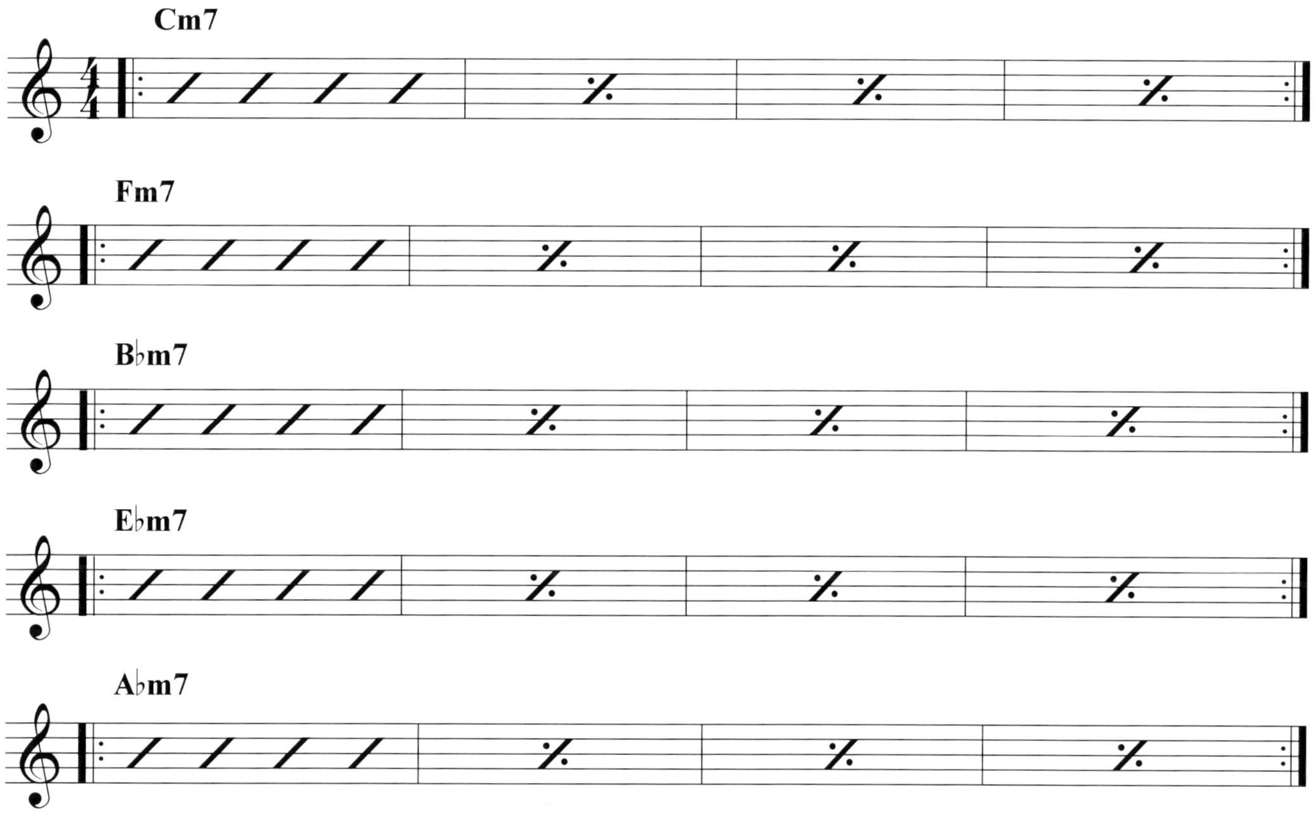

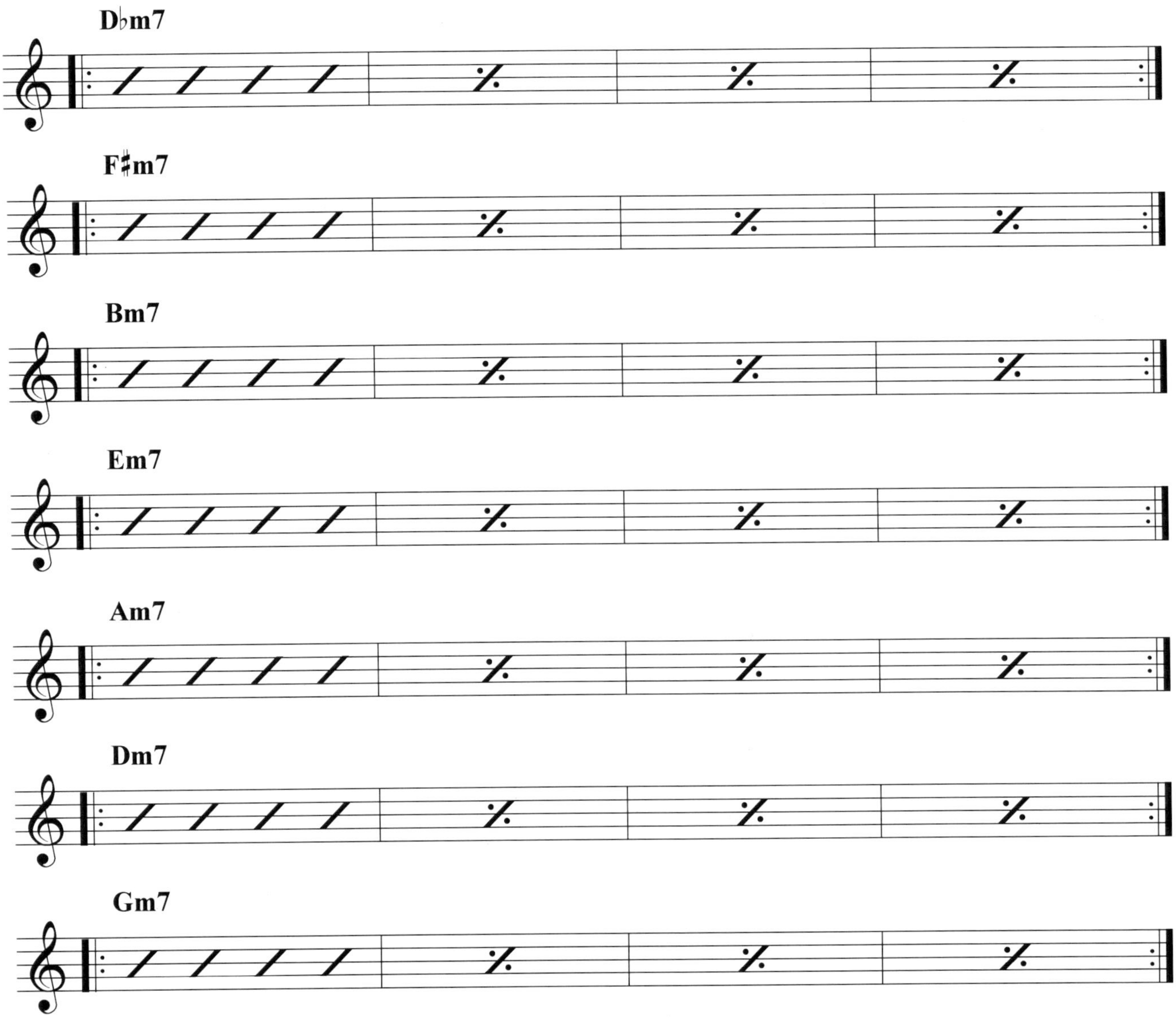

The following exercise makes use of the D Phrygian mode.

CD #8

Lydian Mode

The Lydian mode is the same as a major scale with a raised fourth degree. The C Lydian mode contains the notes: C, D, E, F♯, G, A, and B. It can also be thought of as the mode that begins on a major scale's fourth degree. An F Lydian mode contains the same notes as a C major scale.

C Major **C Lydian**

F Lydian

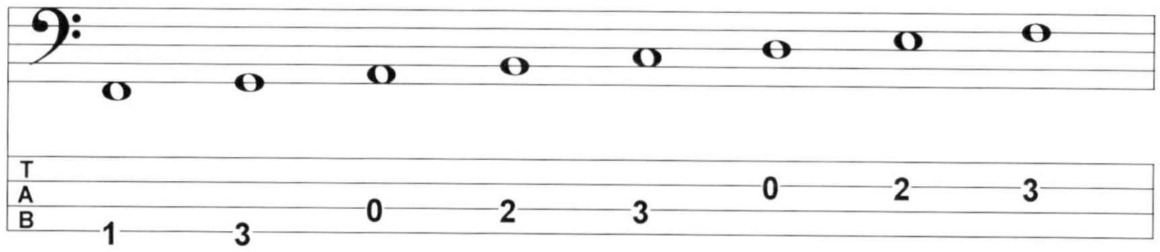

The Lydian mode works against major chords and their basic embellishments (sixth, major seventh, etc.). It is most effective when used against major seventh sharp eleven chords (maj. 7♯11). The construction of this mode, as well as the fourth string linear diagram of this mode with an F as the root, are shown below. Also, one-octave and two-octave patterns are given. Make sure one-octave patterns can be played in all twelve keys before moving on to two-octave patterns. Use the rhythm track provided to master these one-octave and two-octave Lydian mode patterns. Use scalar patterns to solidify the mastery of this mode.

Construction: whole step, whole step, whole step, half step, whole step, whole step, half step

F Lydian

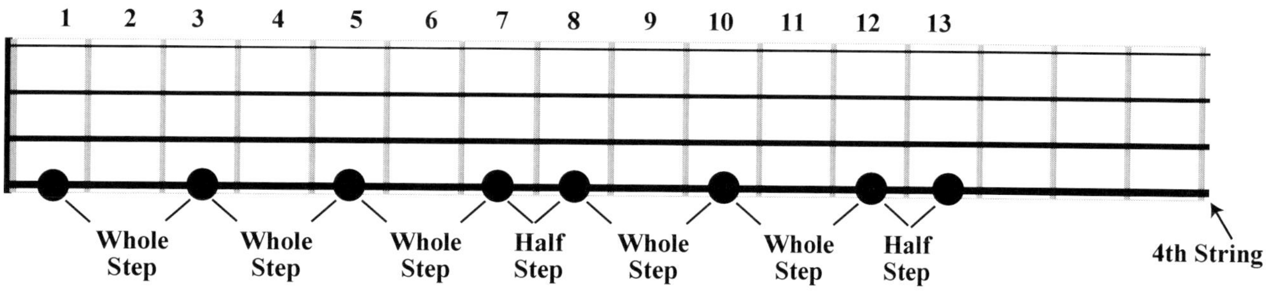

One-Octave Patterns - Lydian

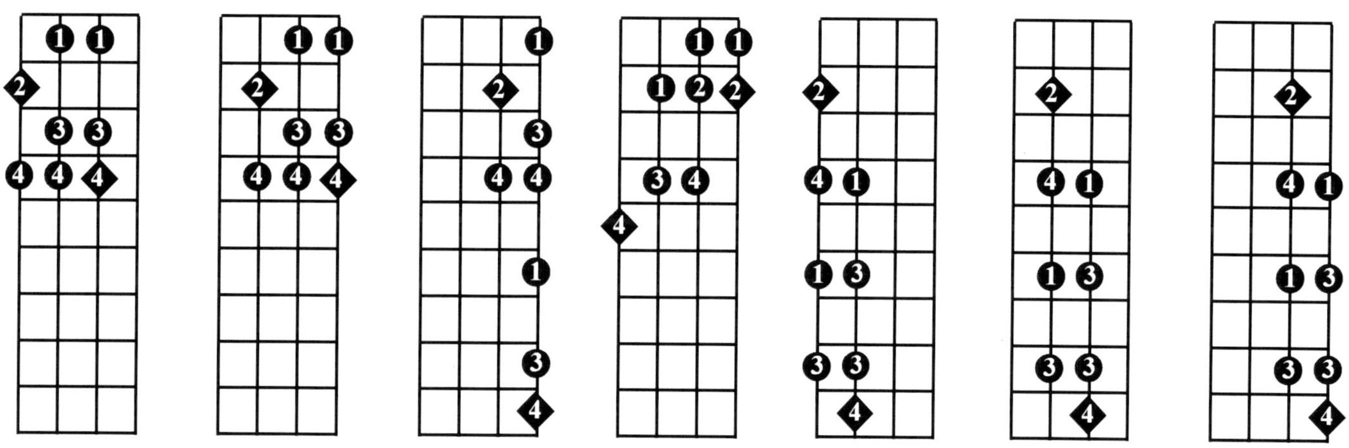

Two-Octave Patterns – Lydian

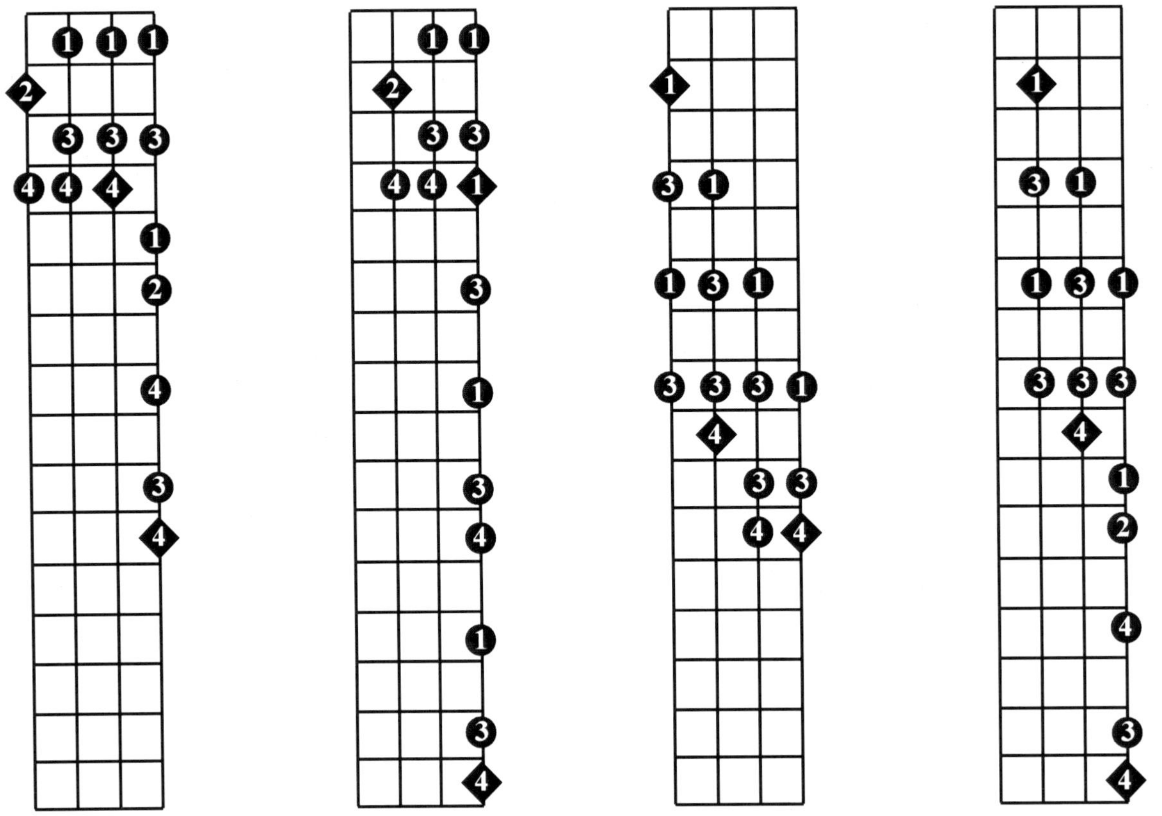

CD #9 (also try with #2)

The following exercise makes use of the G Lydian mode.

CD #10

Mixolydian Mode

The Mixolydian mode contains the same intervallic structure as a major scale with the exception of a flatted seventh degree. The C Mixolydian mode contains the notes: C, D, E, F, G, A and B♭. The Mixolydian mode starts and ends on the fifth degree of a major scale. Thus, the G Mixolydian mode contains the same notes as a C major scale.

C Major **C Mixolydian**

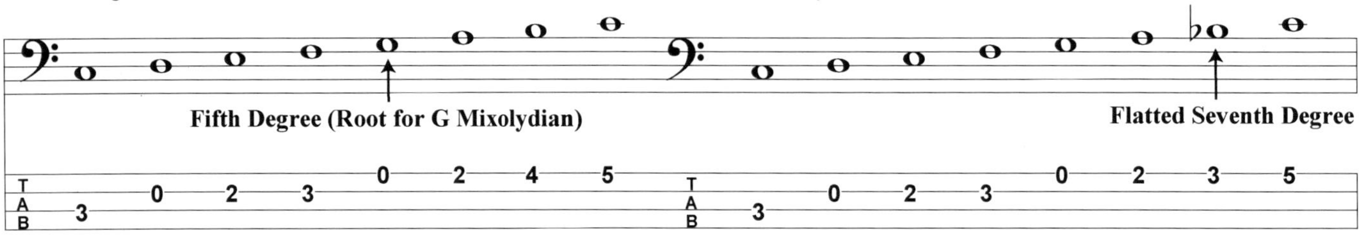

G Mixolydian

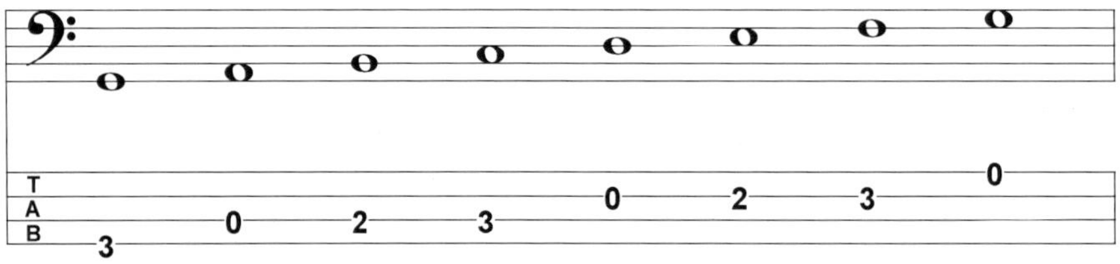

The intervallic make-up, fourth string linear diagram for the key of F showing whole step and half step relationships, and one-octave and two-octave finger patterns of the Mixolydian mode are given below.

Construction: whole step, whole step, half step, whole step, whole step, half step, whole step

F Mixolydian

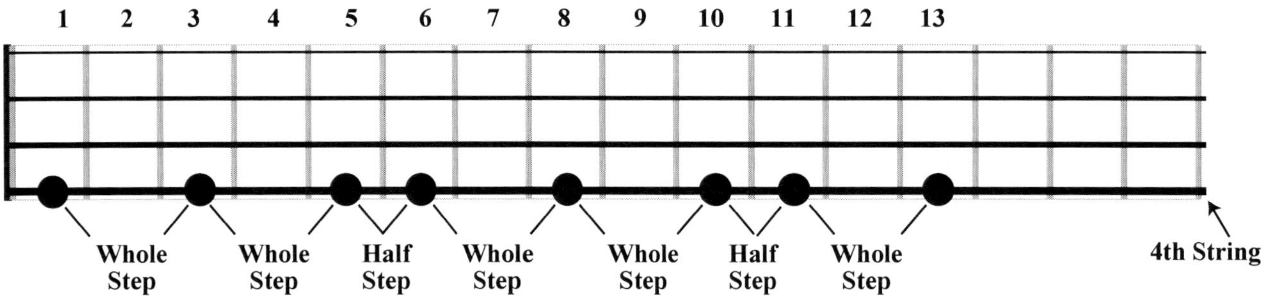

One-Octave Patterns - Mixolydian

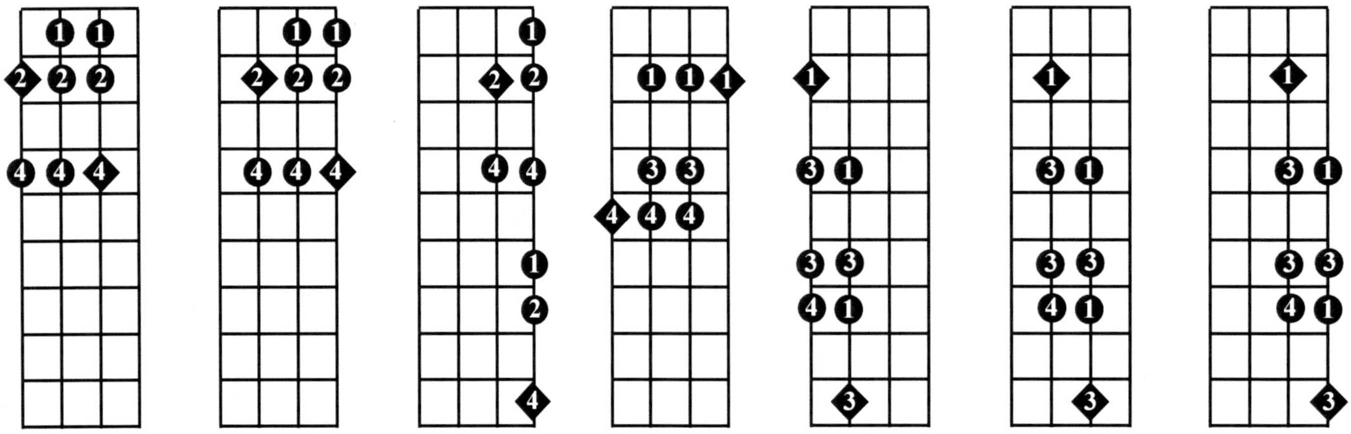

Two-Octave Patterns – Mixolydian

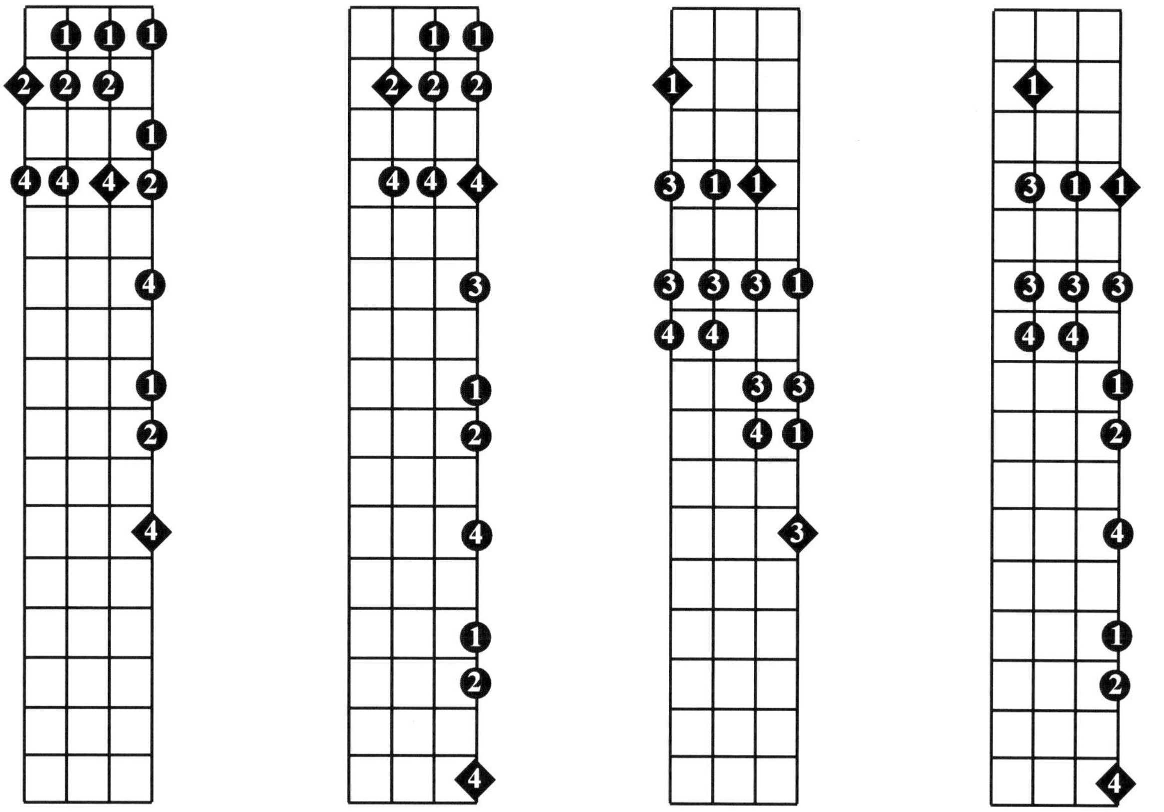

This mode should be used to improvise against dominant seventh, eleventh (This chord may be written at times as a 7sus chord.), ninth, and thirteenth chords. Following the practice regimen given for the other scales and modes, master this scale in all twelve keys using the following rhythm track that moves around the circle of fourths.

CD #11

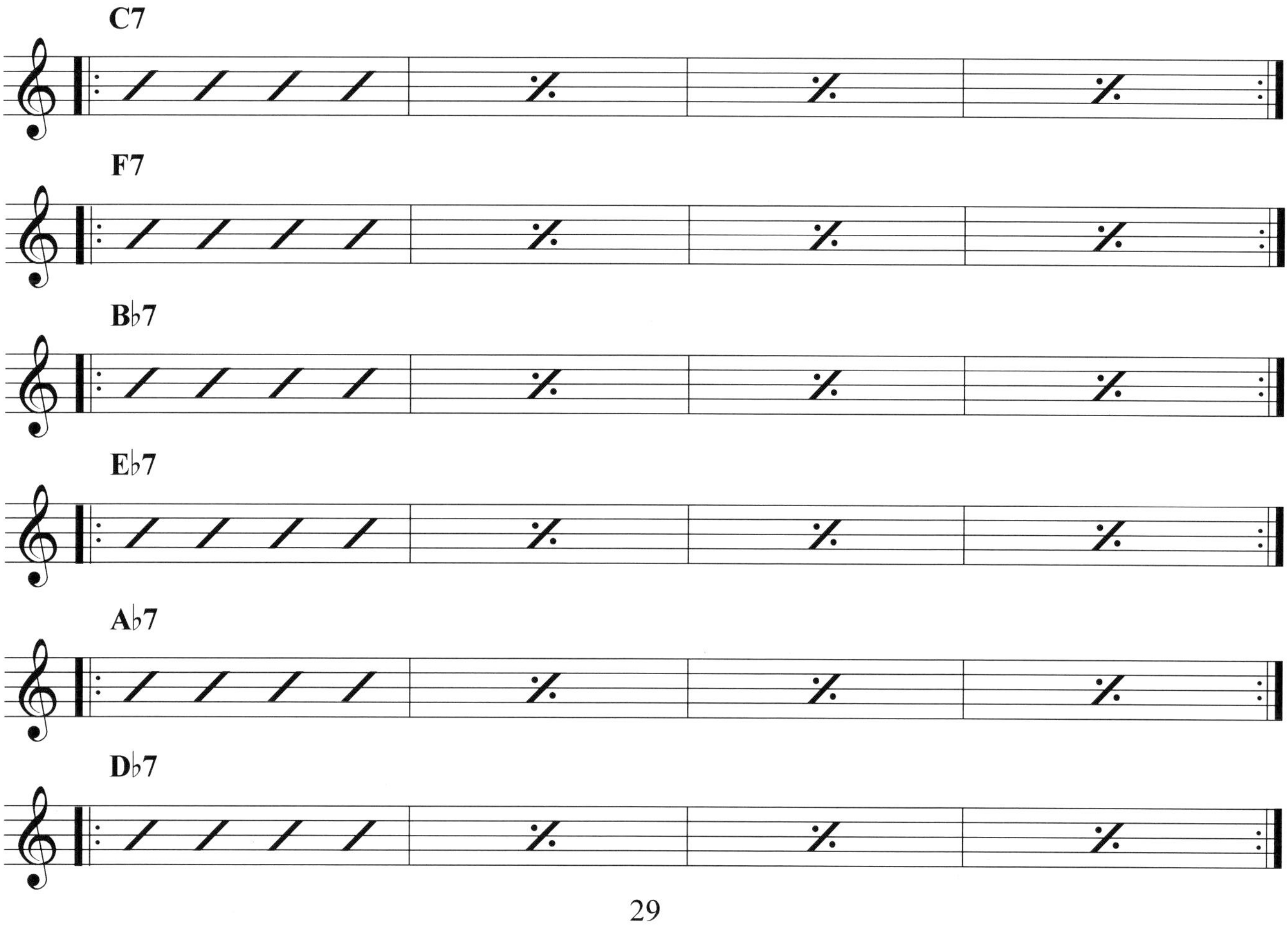

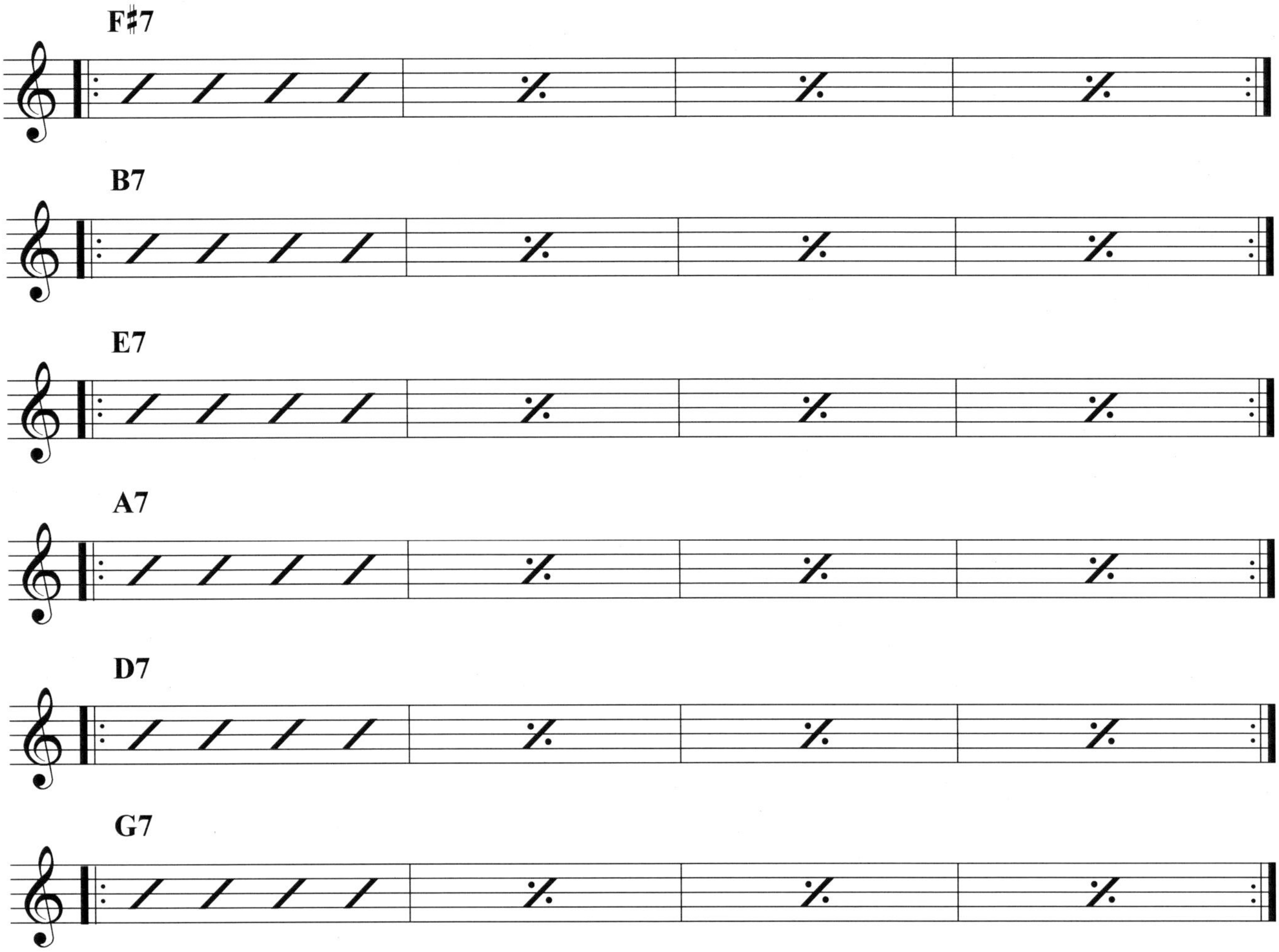

The following exercise makes use of the B♭ Mixolydian mode.

CD #12

Locrian Mode

The Locrian mode is the final mode derived from the major scale. Its root note is the seventh step of a major scale. The B Locrian mode contains the same notes as a C major scale. The locrian mode may also be viewed as a natural minor scale with lowered second and fifth degrees. The notes found in the A Locrian mode are: A, B♭, C, D, E♭, F, G (the same notes as a B♭ major scale).

C Major **B Locrian**

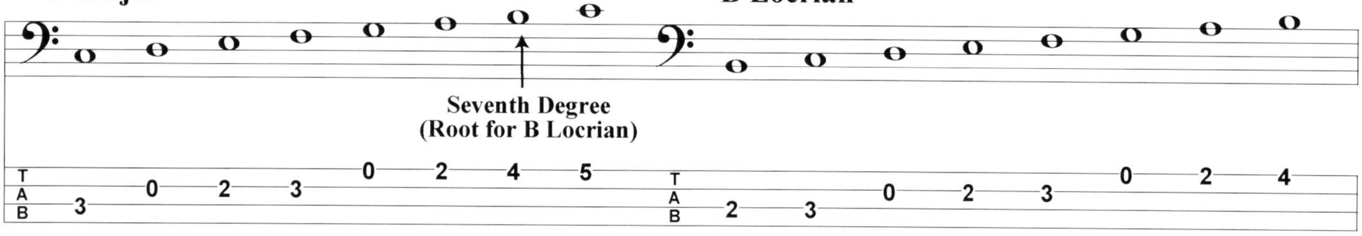

A Natural Minor (Aeolian) **A Locrian**

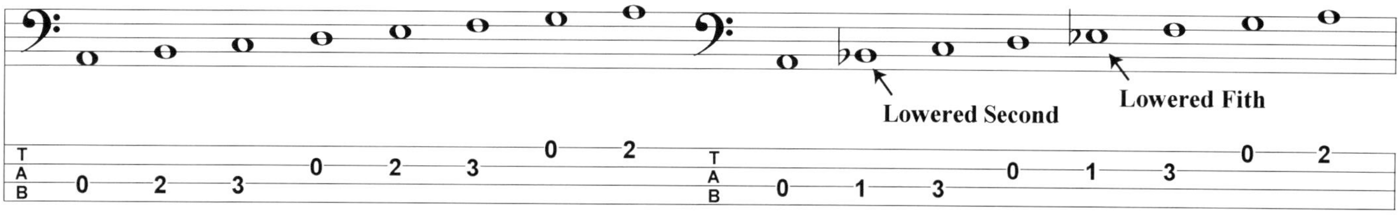

The Locrian mode's construction in whole steps and half steps and a linear diagram for the F Locrian mode on the fourth string are given below. As with the other modes, one-octave and two-octave finger patterns are shown below. Be sure to practice this scale in every position given and in every key.

Construction: half step, whole step, whole step, half step, whole step, whole step, whole step

F Locrian

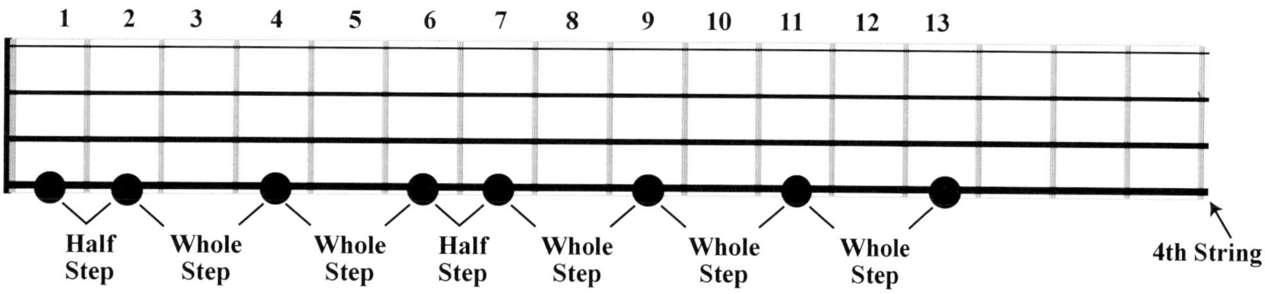

One-Octave Patterns - Locrian

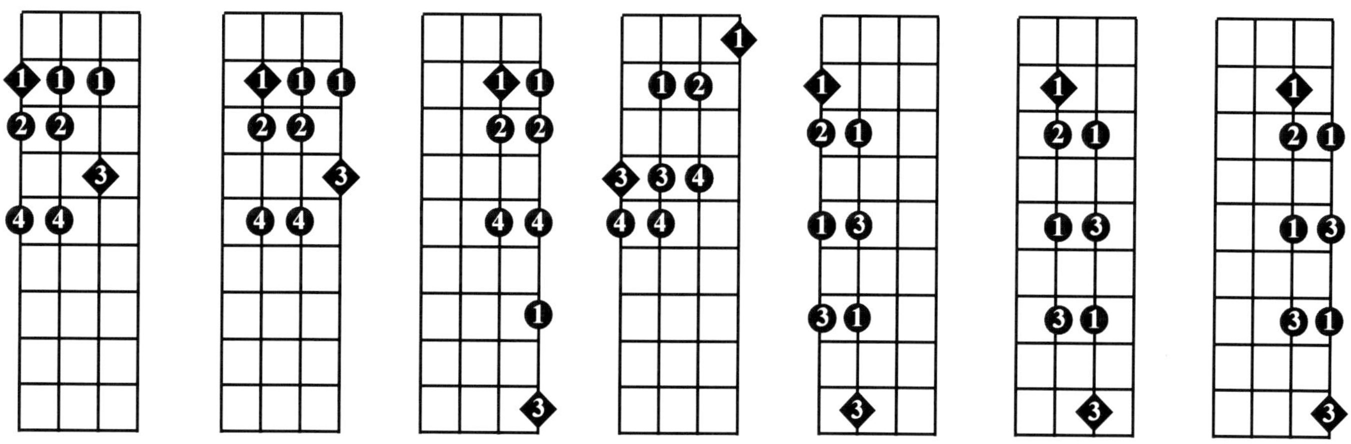

Two-Octave Patterns – Locrian

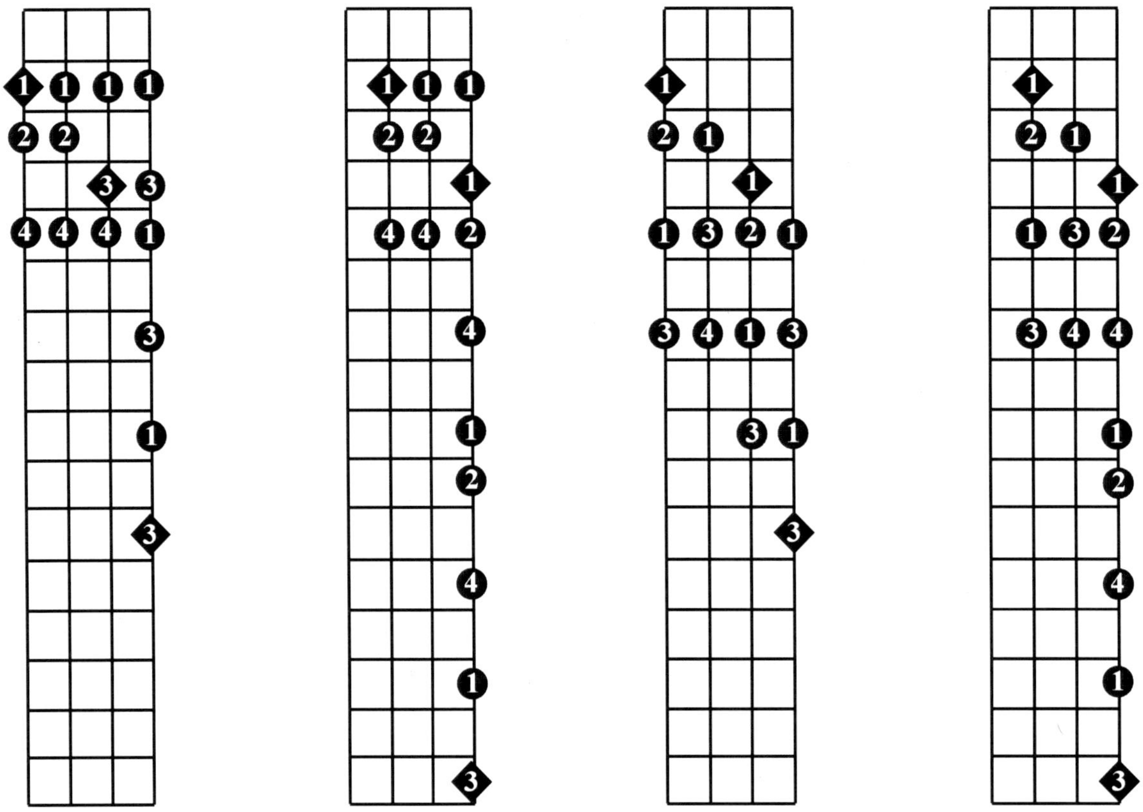

Because this mode has minor qualities and a flatted fifth degree, it works nicely against minor seven, flat-five chords (m7♭5). Another name for this chord is the half-diminished chord (ø7). Use the following rhythm tracks to practice this mode around the circle of fourths. Make sure to practice this mode ascending and descending, as well as scalar patterns, to ensure complete mastery.

CD #13

Cm7♭5

Fm7♭5

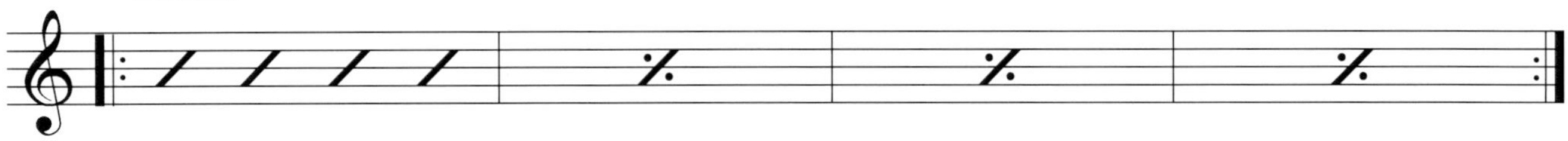

B♭m7♭5

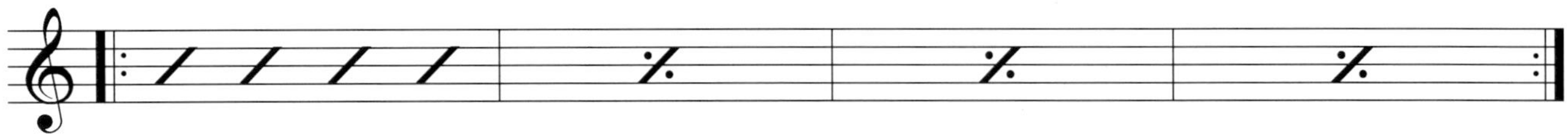

E♭m7♭5

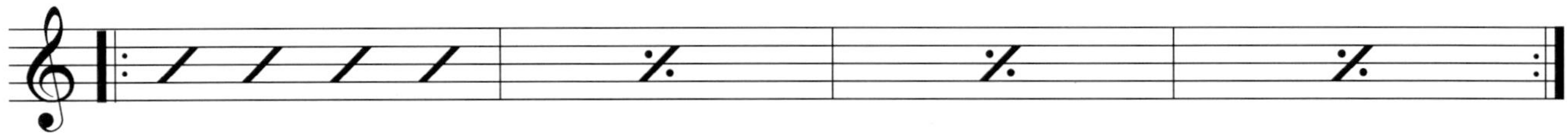

A♭m7♭5

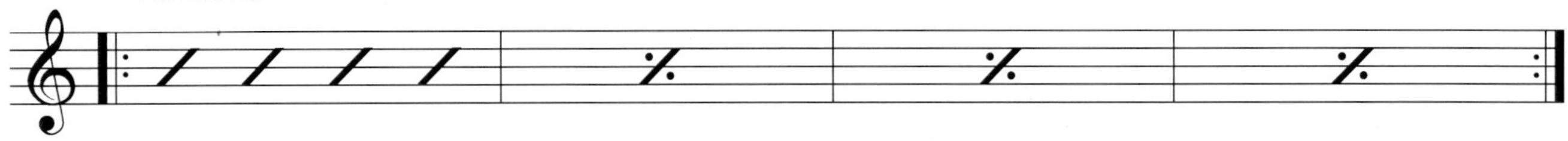

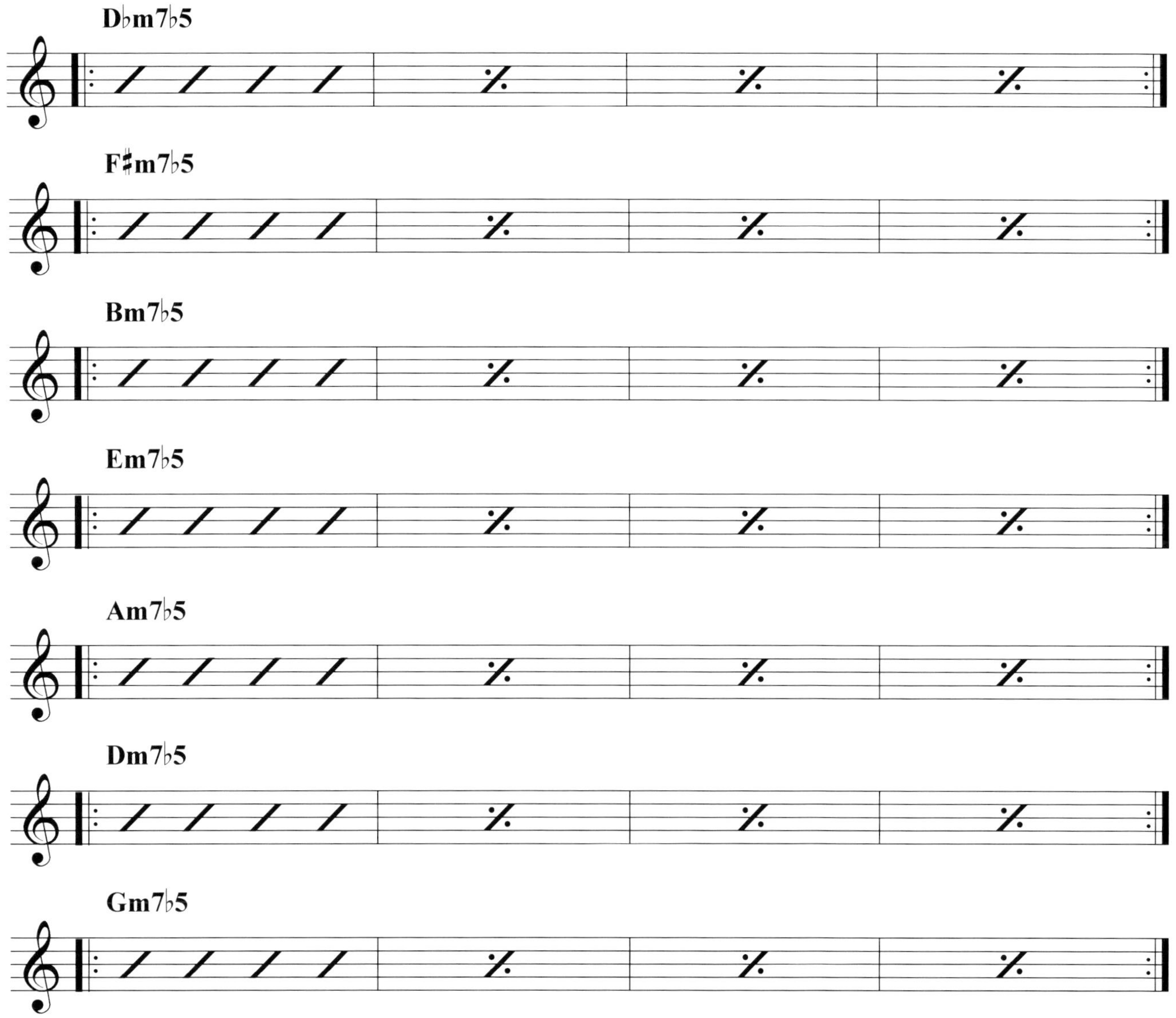

The following exercise makes use of the D Locrian mode.

CD #14

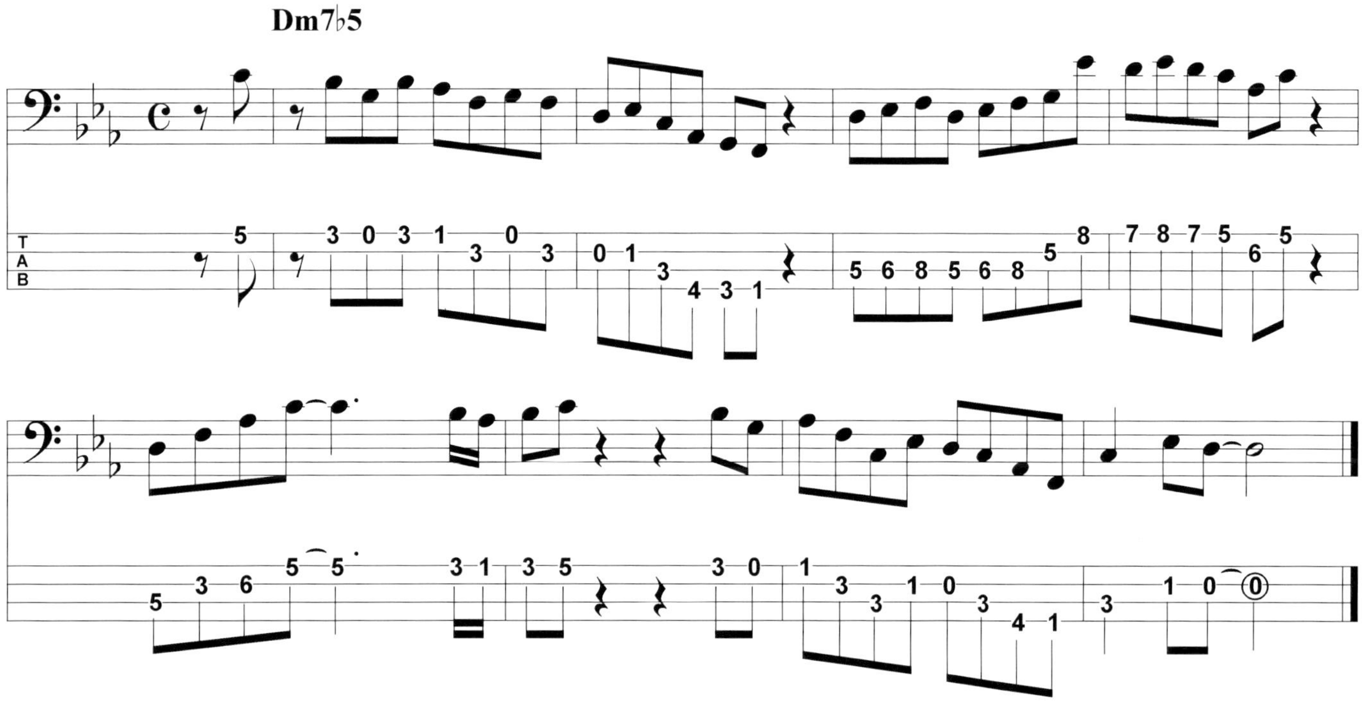

Harmonic, Melodic and Jazz Melodic Minor Scales

Harmonic, Melodic and Jazz Melodic Minor Scales

As stated earlier, the natural scale is exactly the same as the Aeolian mode. The construction of the natural minor scale is the same as a major scale, but the third, sixth, and seventh degrees are lowered. There are two other scales that are closely related to the natural minor scale that are used in jazz improvisation. These are the harmonic minor and the melodic minor scales. The harmonic minor scale is a natural minor scale with a raised seventh degree. The raised seventh degree is called the "leading tone" because it leads chromatically to the root of the scale. The harmonic minor scale is shown below.

Traditionally, the melodic minor scale is a natural minor scale with raised sixth and seventh degrees when it is played ascending, but the notes of the natural minor scale are used when it is played descending. Classical music generally uses the ascending and descending patterns, but in jazz only the ascending pattern is used regardless of which direction the scale is played. While the melodic minor is shown below and is covered later in this chapter, only the nontraditional (ascending only) pattern of this scale should be used as an improvisatory tool.

A Natural Minor (Aeolian Mode) **A Harmonic Minor**

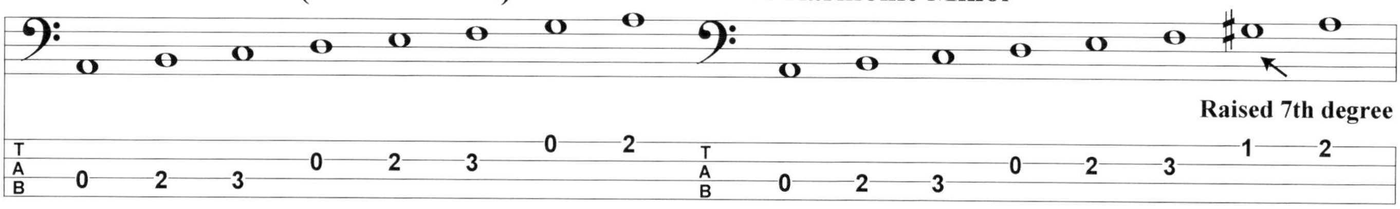

A Melodic Minor **Natural Minor Descending**

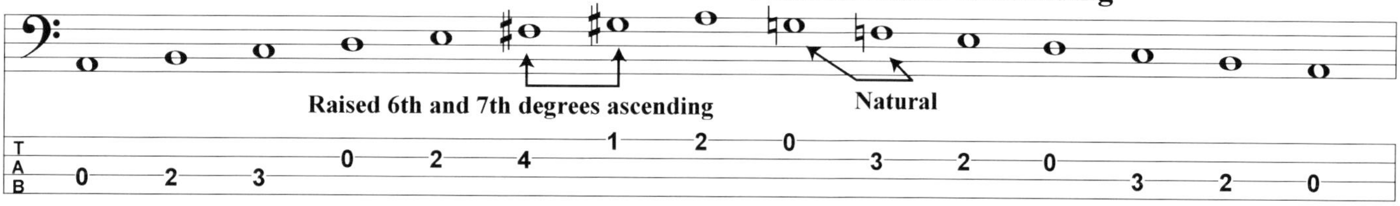

A Jazz Melodic Minor

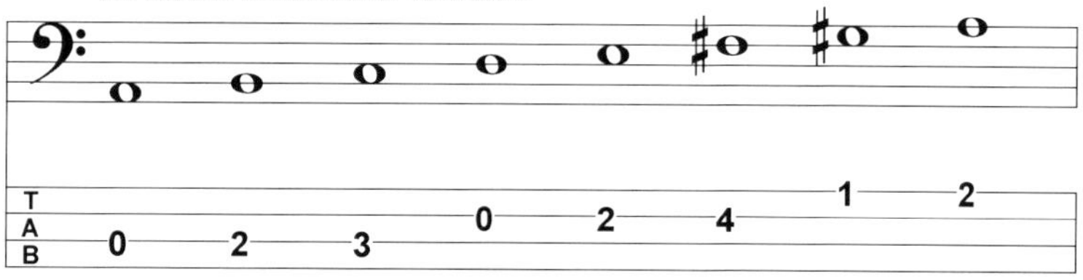

Even though the harmonic and melodic minor scales are very closely related, they have different sounds, and therefore, will be presented separately in construction, finger patterns, and application. Shown below is the construction in whole steps and half steps of the harmonic minor scale and a linear F harmonic minor scale shown only on the fourth string. (Remember, it is a good idea to play all of the scales and modes on each of the four strings independently so the relationship of whole steps and half step construction may be seen.) One-octave and two-octave finger patterns for this scale are also given. Practice these patterns using sequences and scalar patterns ascending and descending using the recorded rhythm track. Because this scale has a minor quality, it may be used against minor and minor major seventh chords (mM7). It works over minor add nine and minor suspended chords.

Construction: whole step, half step, whole step, whole step, half step, one and a half steps, half step

F Harmonic Minor

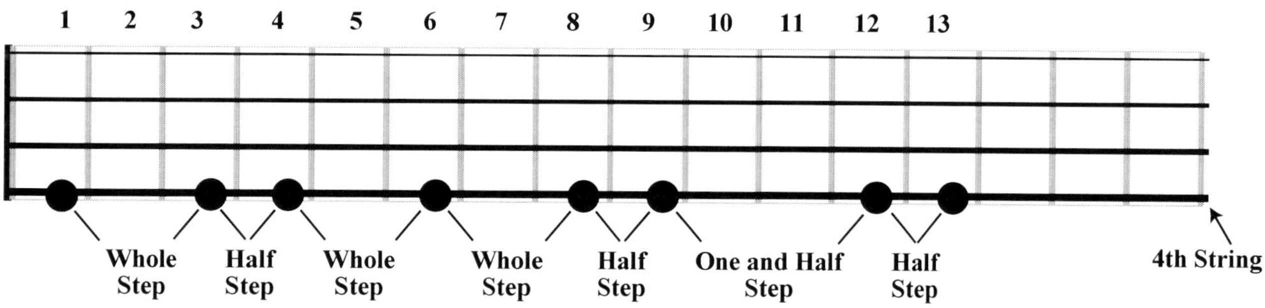

One-Octave Patterns - Harmonic Minor

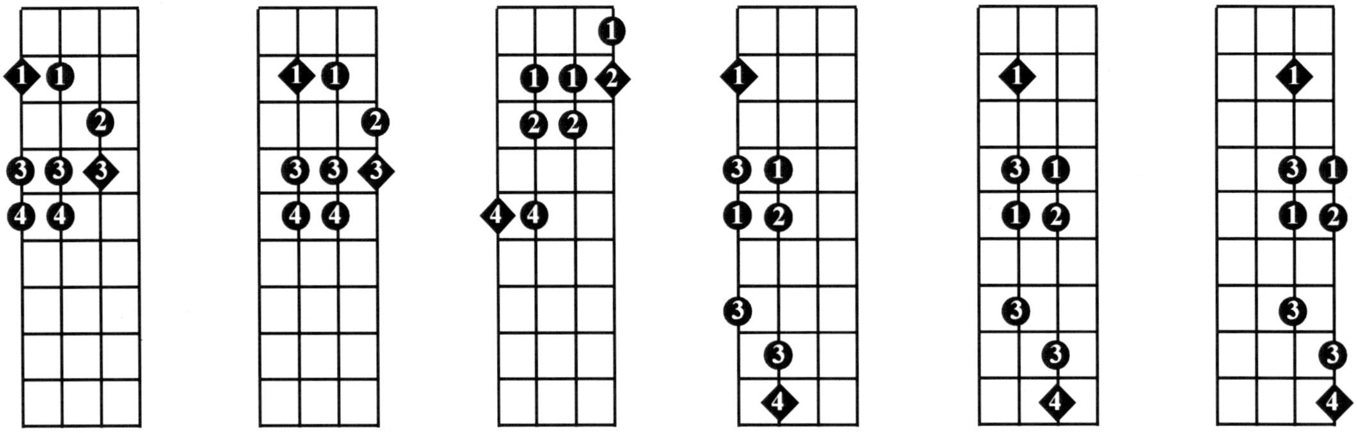

Two-Octave Patterns - Harmonic Minor

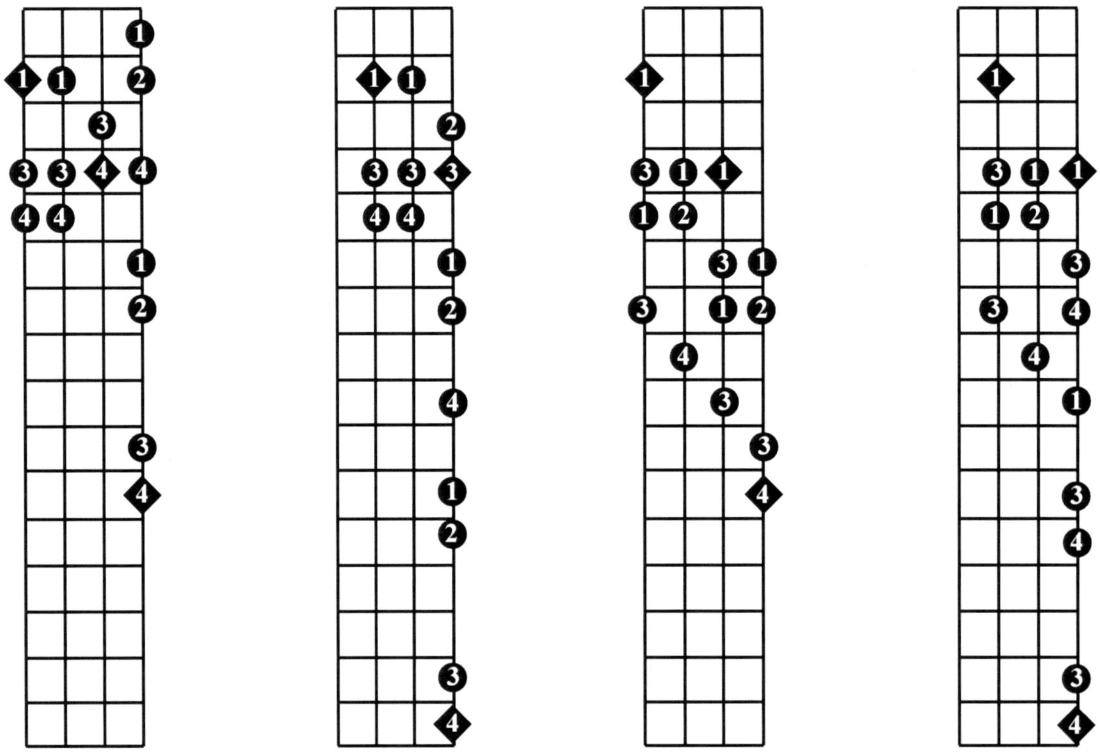

CD #15

Here is an example of how the harmonic minor scale can be used to improvise over minor chords.

CD #16

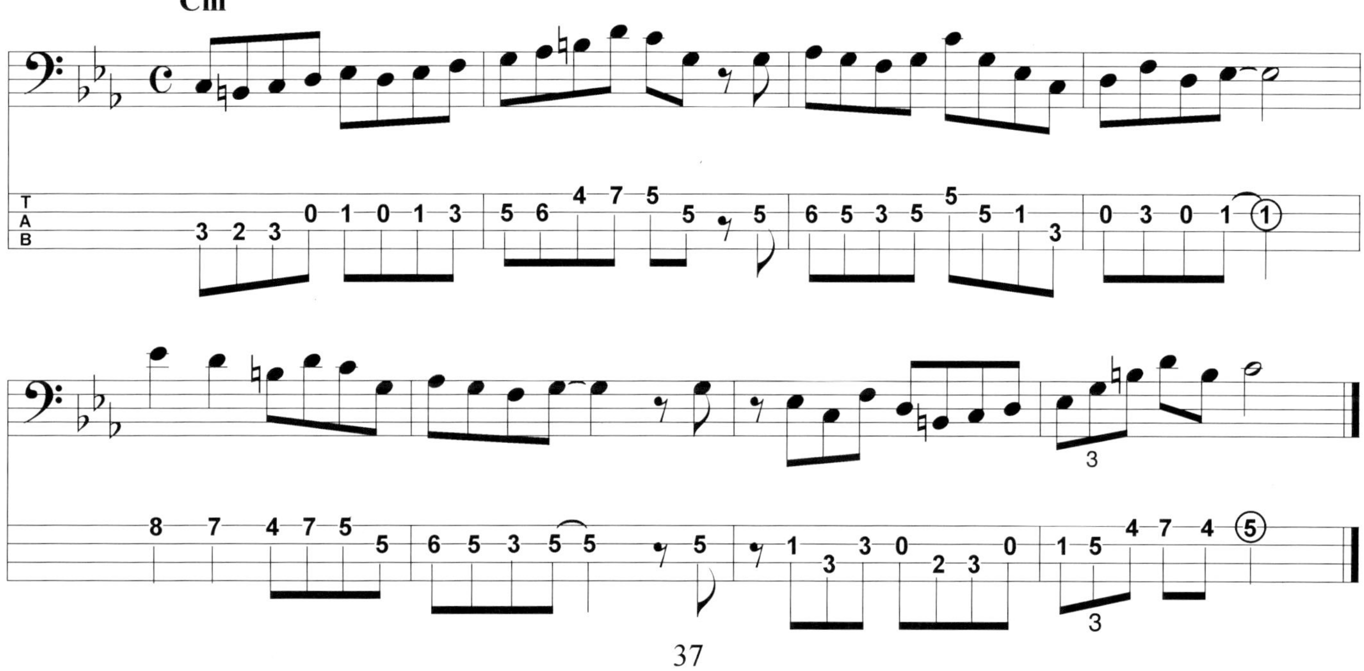

The whole step and half step construction of the melodic minor scale, as well as a linearly constructed F melodic minor scale, is shown below. Ascending pattern notes are solid dots and the descending notes are hollow. One-octave and two-octave finger patterns are also given for the traditional melodic minor scale. Utilizing scalar patterns and sequenced ideas, use the following rhythm track to practice this scale ascending and descending.

Construction: whole step, half step, whole step, whole step, whole step, whole step, half step (ascending). Descending is the same as the natural minor scale.

F Melodic Minor

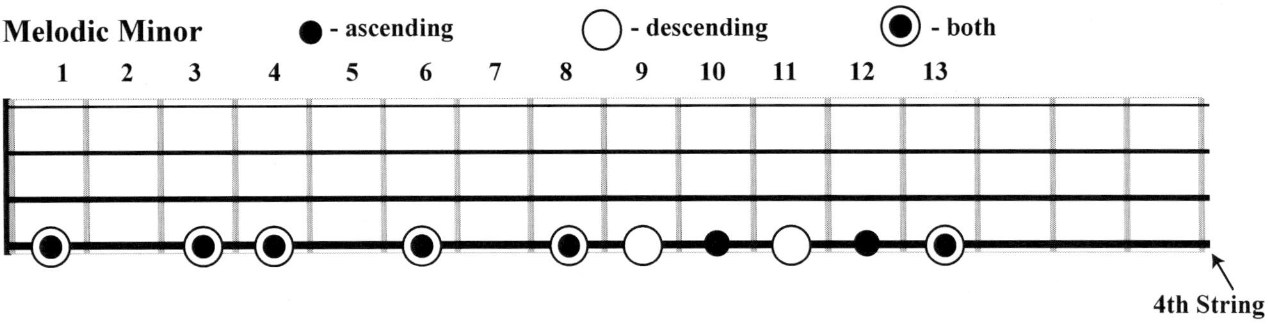

One-Octave Patterns - Melodic Minor

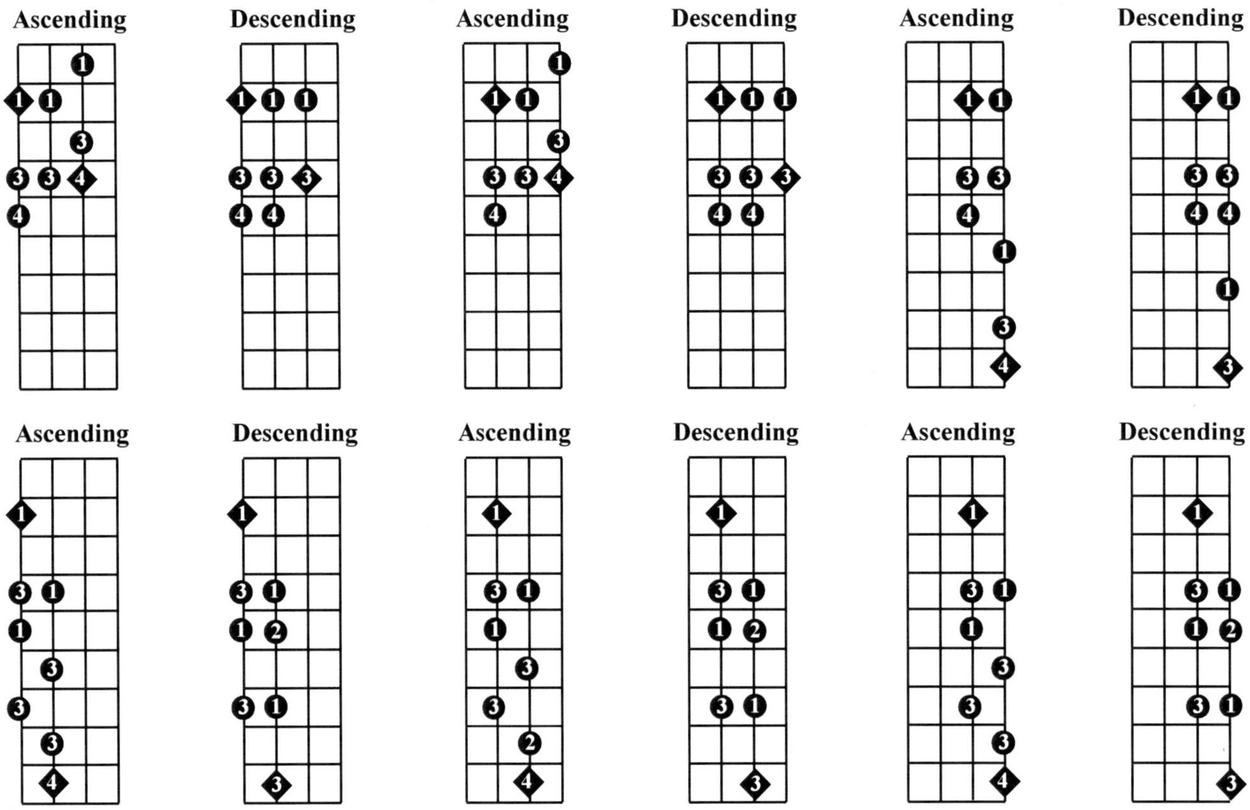

Two-Octave Patterns - Melodic Minor

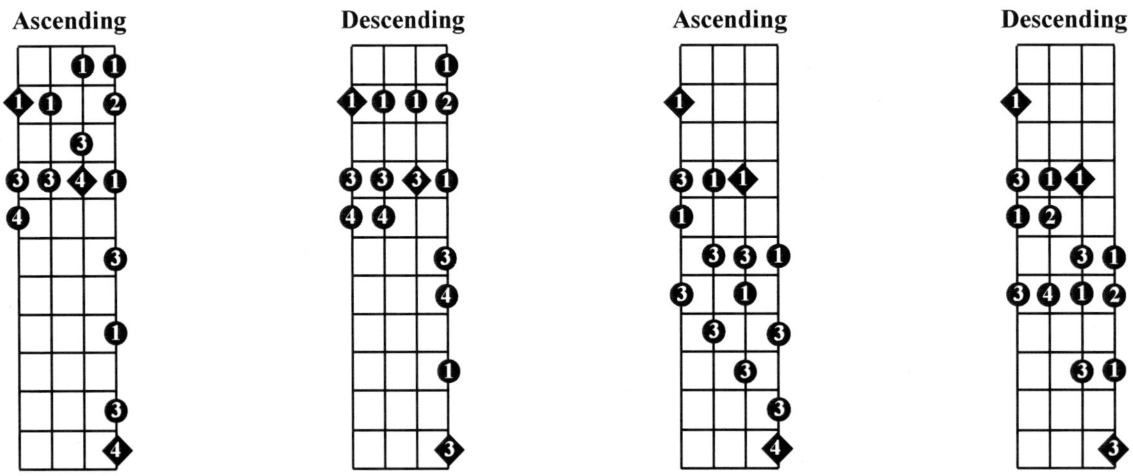

Ascending

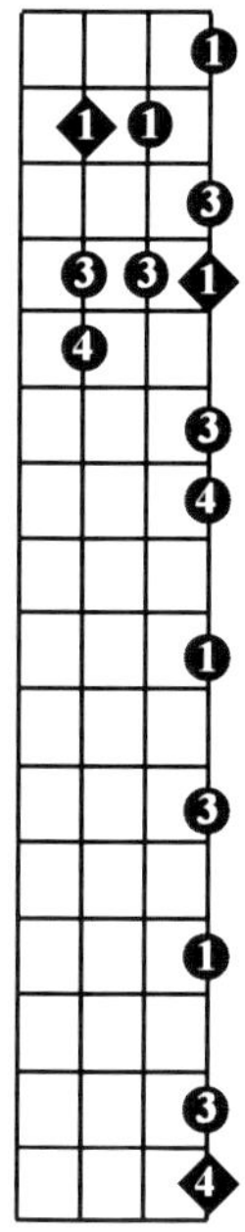

Descending

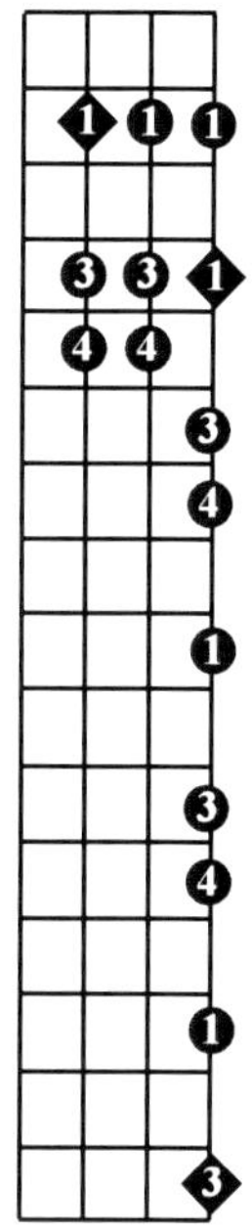

Ascending

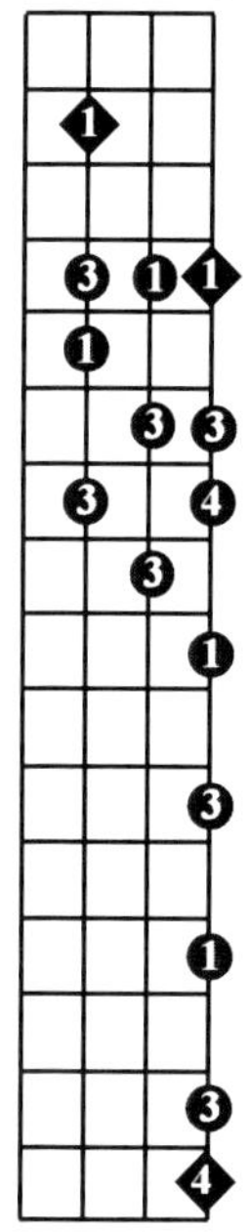

Descending

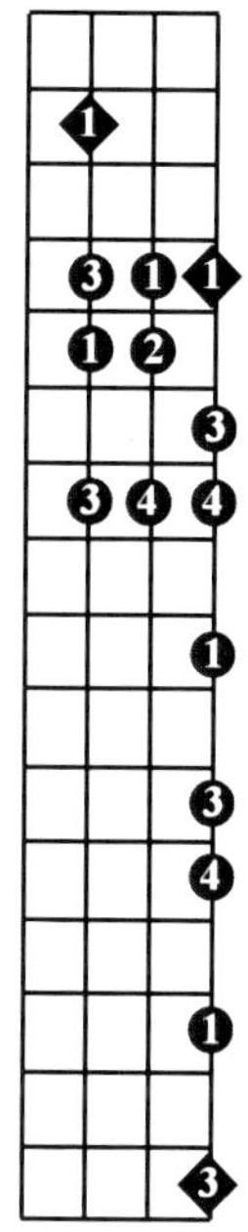

CD #15

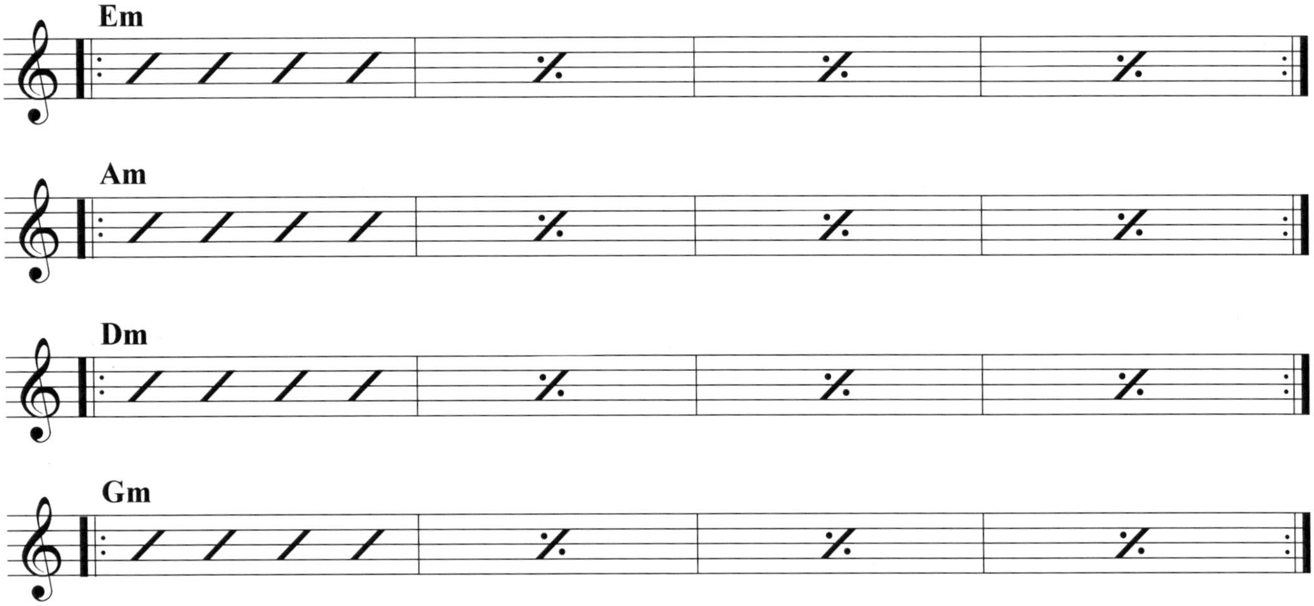

In jazz, as was mentioned earlier, the melodic minor scale is thought of as a natural minor scale with a raised sixth and seventh degree when it is ascending and descending. To master this scale, simply refer to the ascending one-octave and two-octave finger patterns for the melodic minor scale. It may be practiced over the same rhythm track that was provided for the traditional melodic minor scale. Also, this scale works against minor sixth chords.

The following exercise demonstrates how the non-traditional or "jazz" version of the melodic minor scale can be used to improvise over minor chords.

CD #17

Like the major scale, the jazz melodic minor scale contains some very interesting modes, two of which will be covered in depth in the following chapters. The Lydian dominant scale is the fourth mode of the melodic minor and the altered scale is the seventh mode of the melodic minor scale.

Lydian Dominant

The Lydian dominant scale is the Mixolydian mode (often referred to as the dominant scale) with a raised fourth degree. Therefore, the notes which make up the G Lydian dominant are: G, A, B, C♯, D, E, and F. The Lydian dominant scale may also be thought of as the fourth mode of a jazz melodic minor scale. The G Lydian dominant scale and the D jazz melodic minor scale are made up of the same notes.

G Mixolydian **G Lydian Dominant**

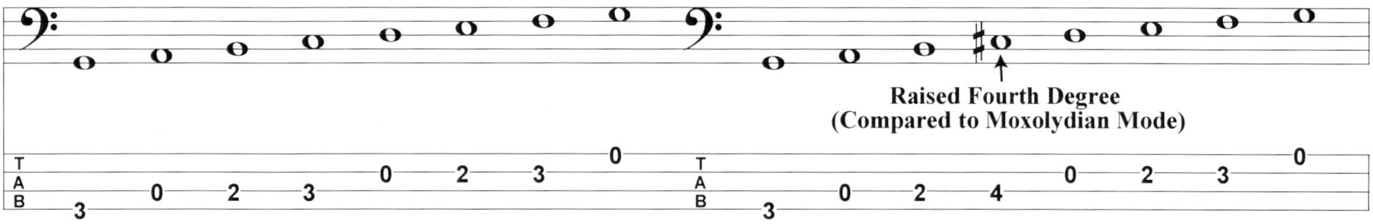

D Melodic Minor **G Lydian Dominant**

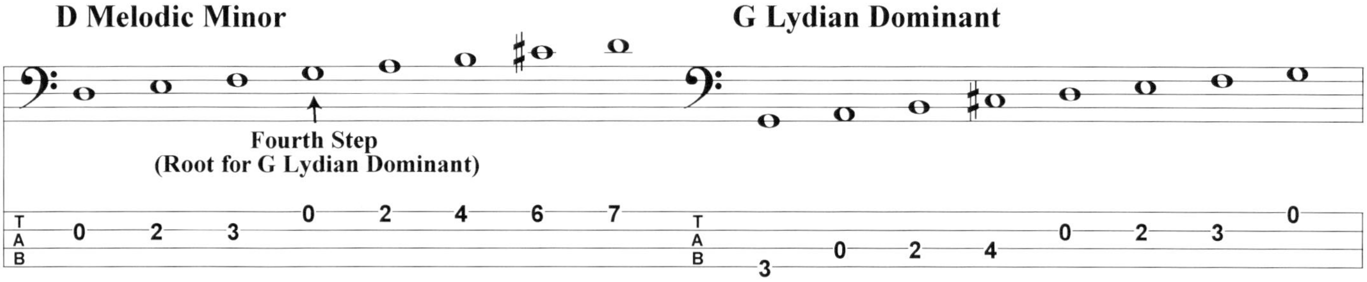

The construction of the Lydian dominant scale with a linear diagram with the root on the fourth string are given below. Remember, it is important to learn all of the scales in this book on one string before practicing vertical finger patterns. By playing the notes on only one string at a time, a better understanding of the fretboard will be gained by each bassist. One-octave and two-octave finger patterns are also given for this scale. Each bassist should make sure to incorporate sequenced scalar patterns when learning this and other scales.

Construction: whole step, whole step, whole step, half step, whole step, half step, whole step

F Lydian Dominant

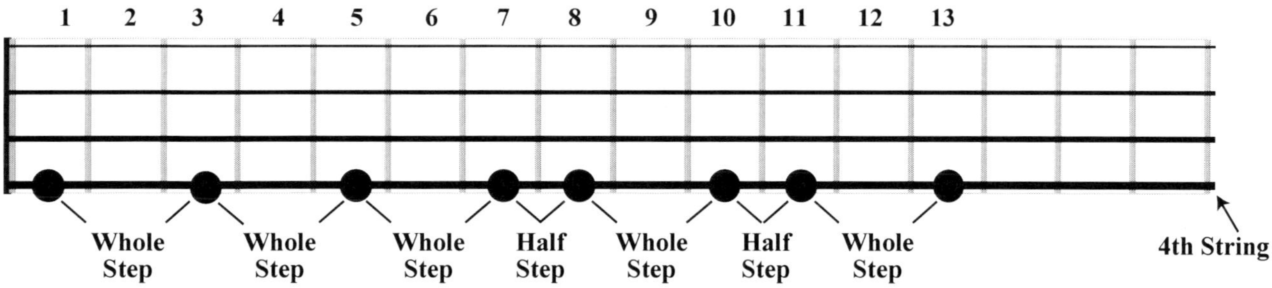

One-Octave Patterns - Lydian Dominant

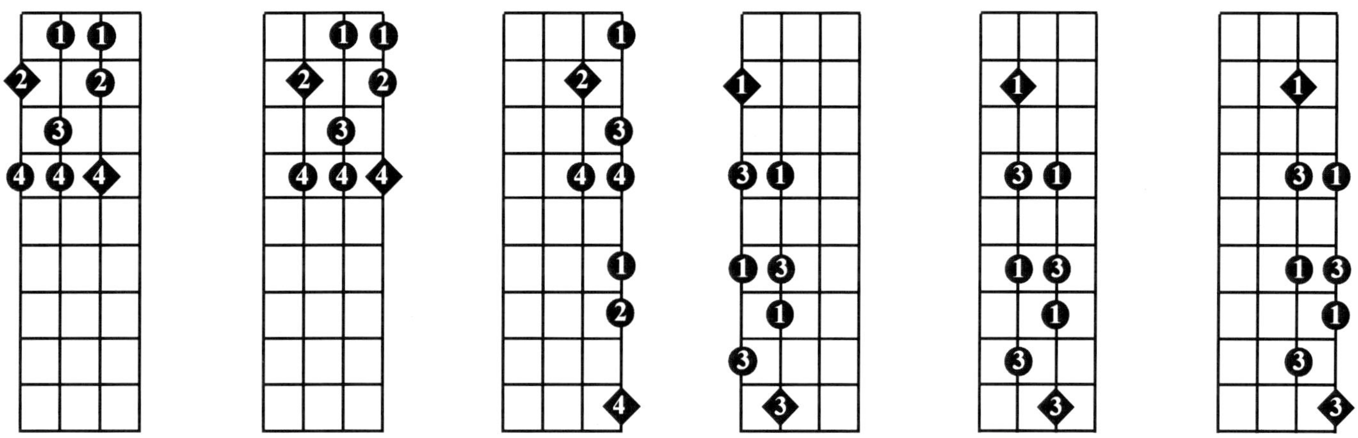

Two-Octave Patterns - Lydian Dominant

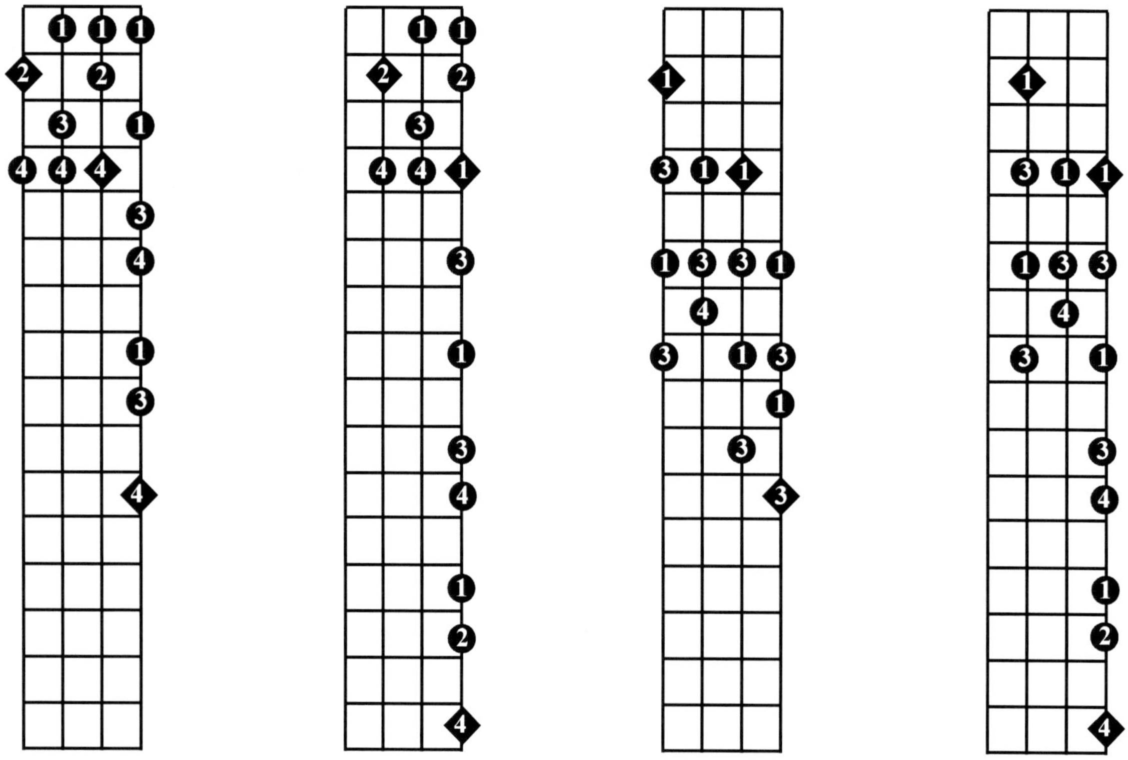

The construction of the Lydian dominant scale makes it an excellent choice when soloing over 7♯11 (7♯4) chords. The sharp eleven or four is the enharmonic equivalent of a flatted fifth. However, a 7♭5 clearly states that the fifth in the chord is to be flatted whereas the 7♯11 indicates the fifth in the chord is natural and the ♯11 is a color tone. The Lydian dominant scale has a ♯4/♯11 but a natural fifth. Special care must be taken when using this scale over 7♭5 chords (avoid playing the natural fifth). Use the following rhythm track which makes use of 7♯11 chords to memorize the Lydian dominant scale.

CD #18

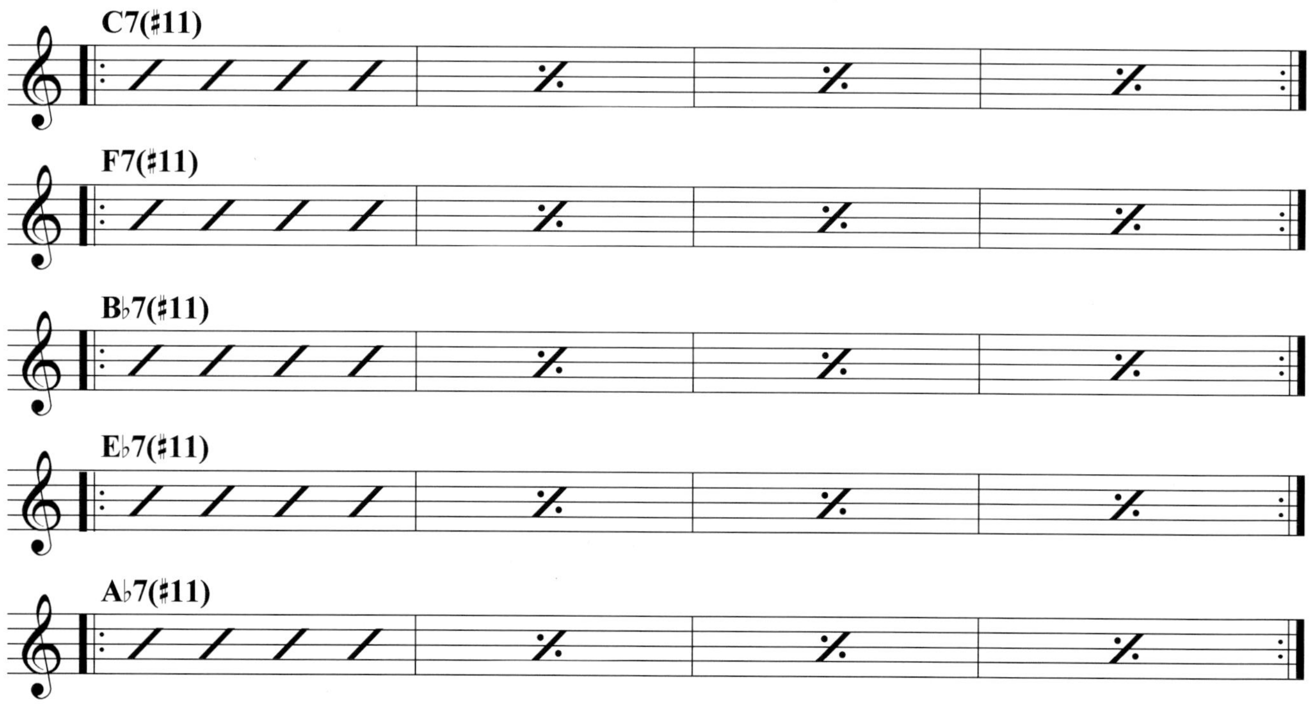

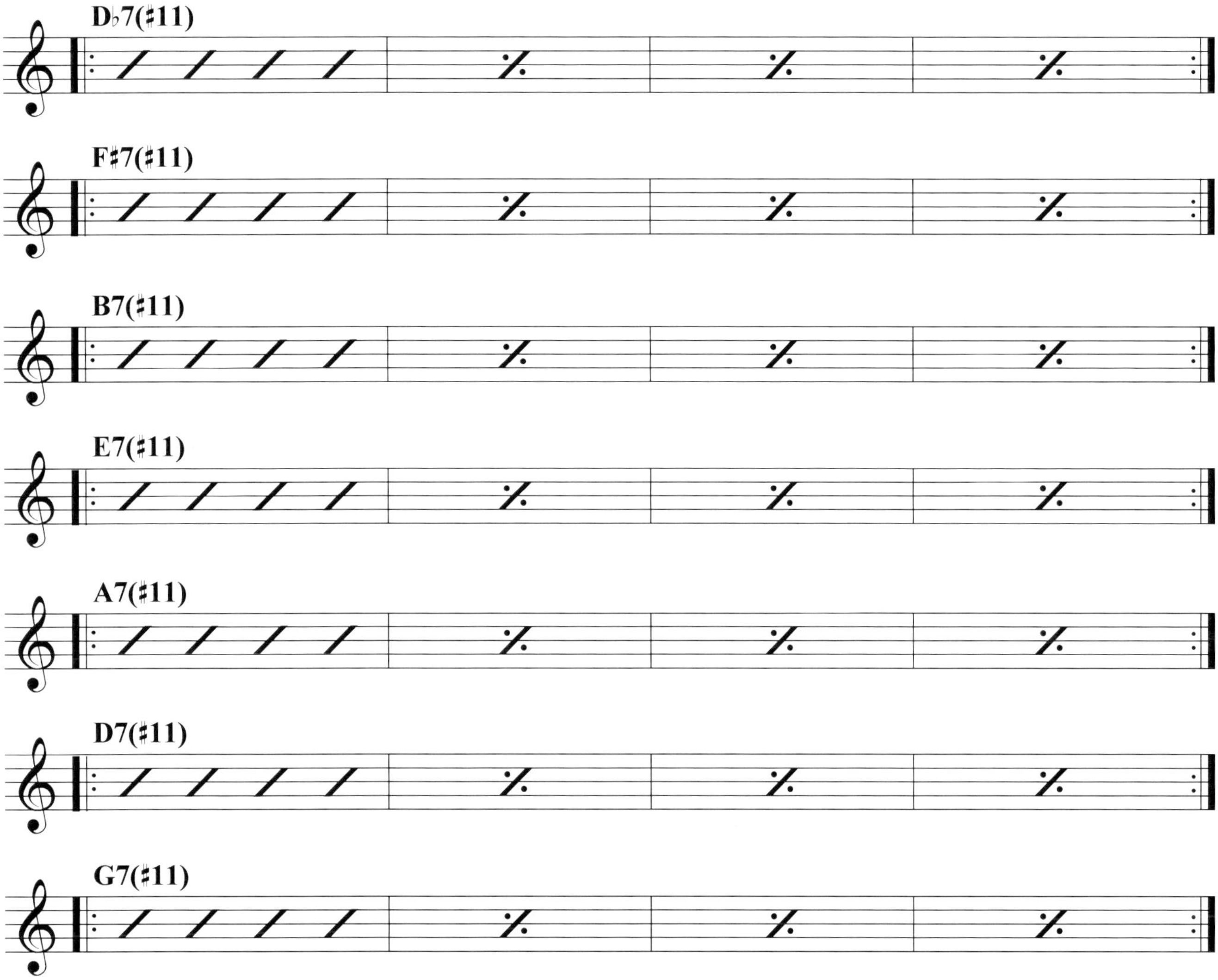

The following exercise demonstrates how the Lydian dominant scale may be used to solo over 7♯11 chords.

CD #19

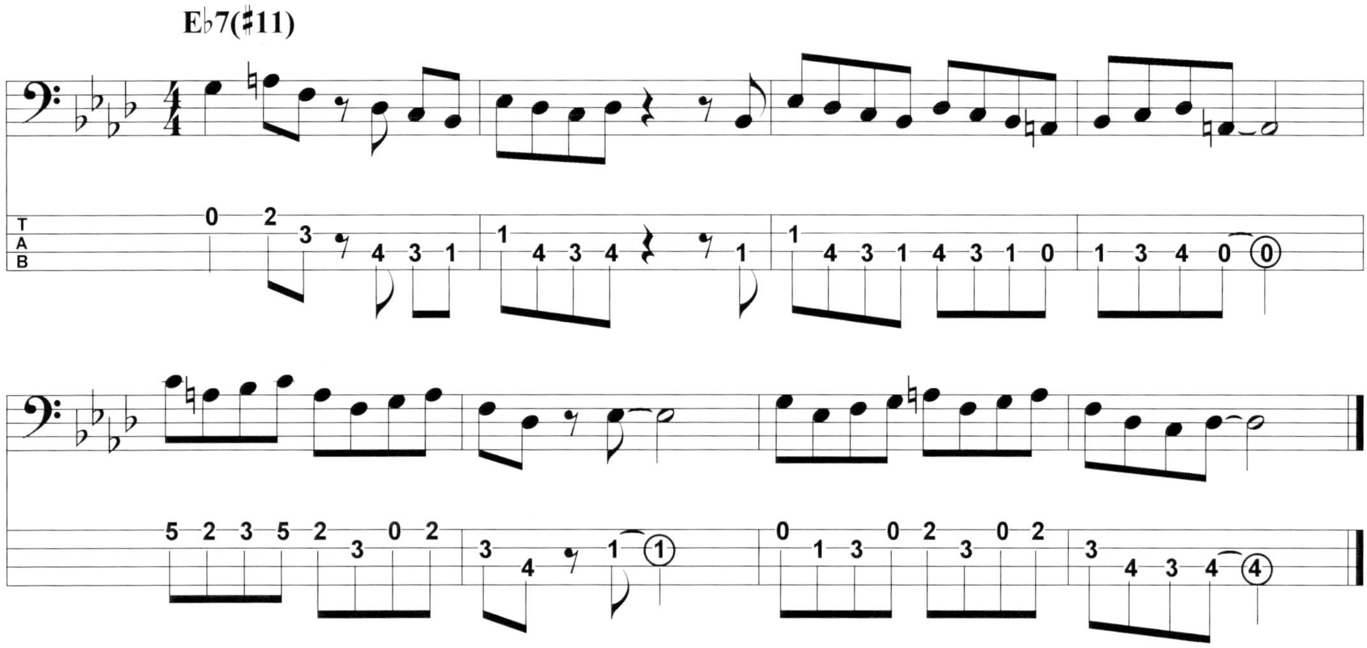

Altered Scale

The altered scale is the seventh mode of a jazz melodic minor scale. An F jazz melodic minor scale contains the E altered scale. Because it is the seventh mode of a jazz melodic minor scale, it is referred to by some musicians as the Super-Locrian mode. It is also referred to by some as the diminished whole-tone scale. This is because the first half of the scale is a diminished scale. (This scale will be discussed in a later chapter.) The second half of the scale is comprised solely of whole-tones. It is called the altered scale because it contains all of the common alterations in a dominant seventh chord. These alterations are the flat and sharp nine (♭9, ♯9) and flat and sharp five (♭5, ♯5). The enharmonic equivalents of the flat five and sharp five are the sharp eleven (♯11) and the flat thirteen (♭13), respectively. The C altered scale is shown below compared to a C major scale. This comparison makes it clearer why it is referred to as the altered scale.

F Melodic Minor **E Altered Scale**

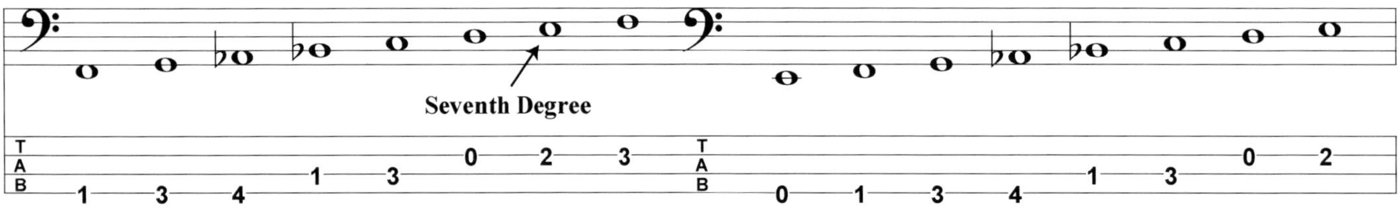

C Major Scale **C Altered Scale**

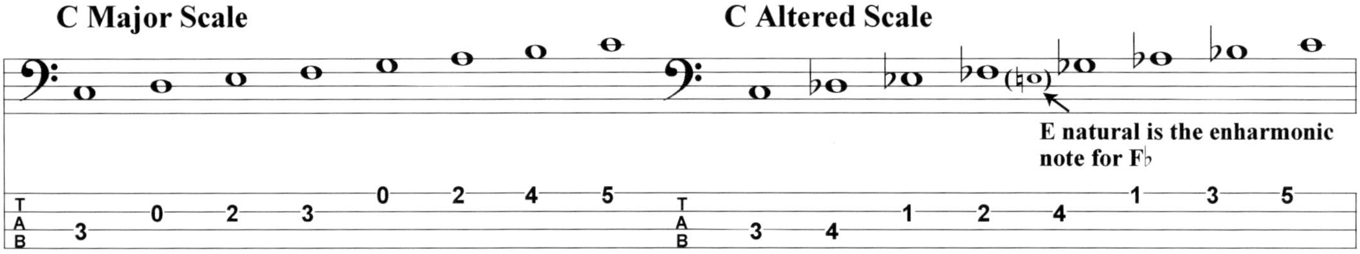

The altered scale construction in whole steps and half steps with linear diagram showing the root on the fourth string is given below. One-octave and two-octave finger patterns are also given.

Construction: half step, whole step, half step, whole step, whole step, whole step, whole step

F Altered Scale

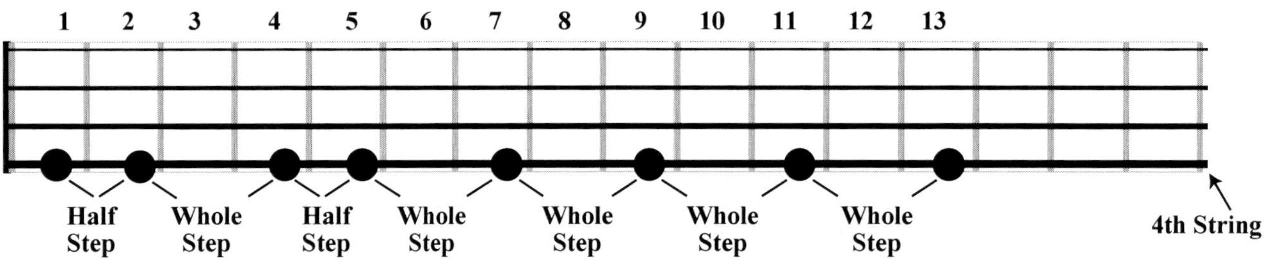

One-Octave Patterns - Altered Scale

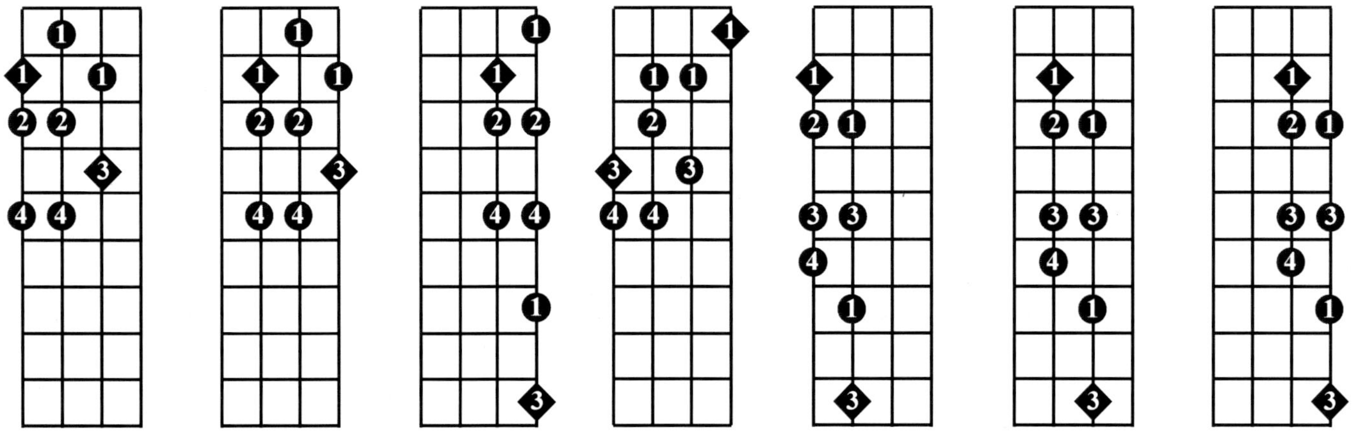

Two-Octave Patterns - Altered Scale

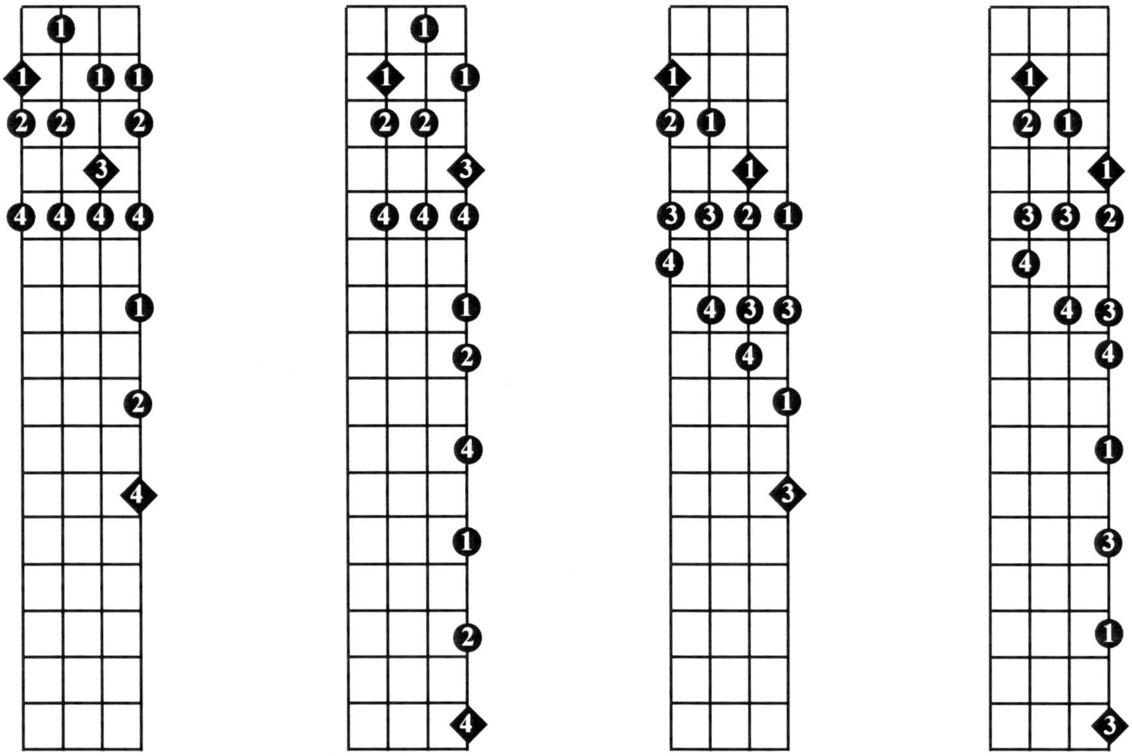

Because this scale contains so many alterations, it works well against any kind of dominant seven altered chord such as 7♭5, 7♯5, 7♭9, 7♯9, and any combinations of these alterations (7♯5♭9 or 7♭5♭9 etc.). For this reason, the rhythm track provided for practicing this scale contains many different altered seventh chords. There are many applications for this scale. Have fun exploring and finding uses for this scale.

CD #20

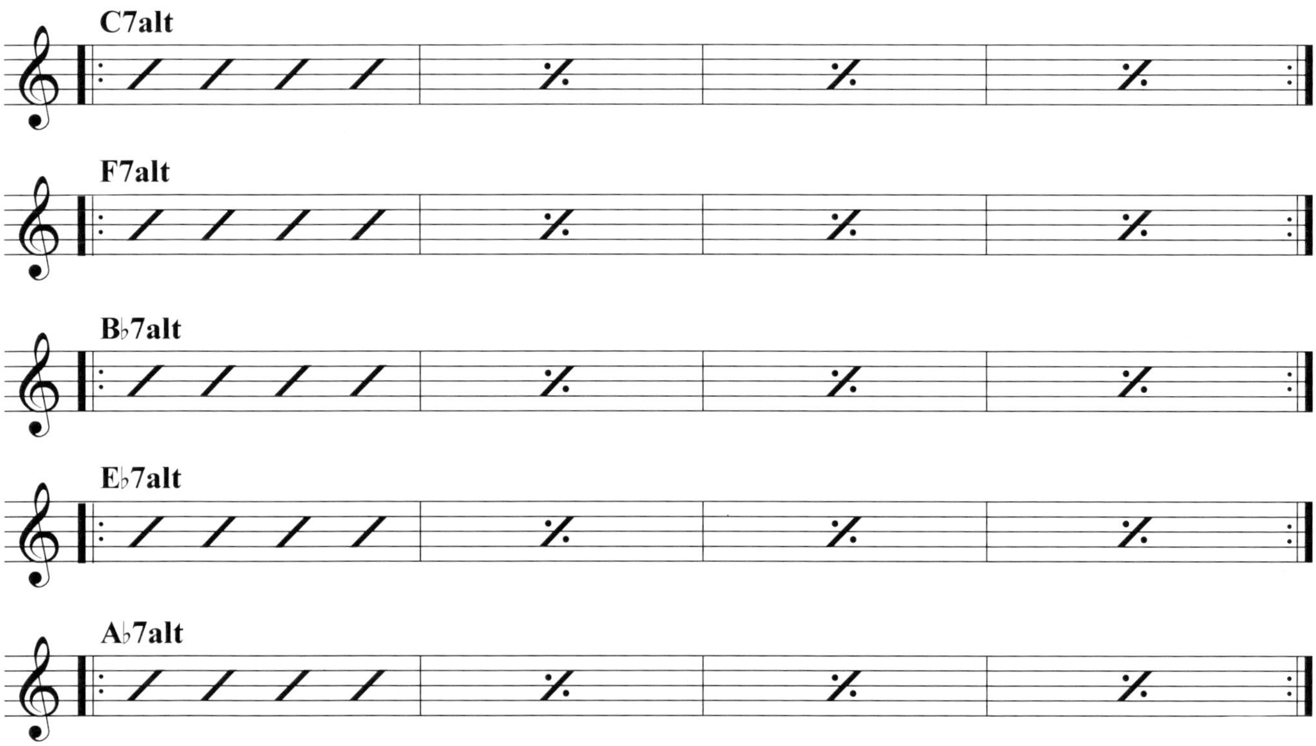

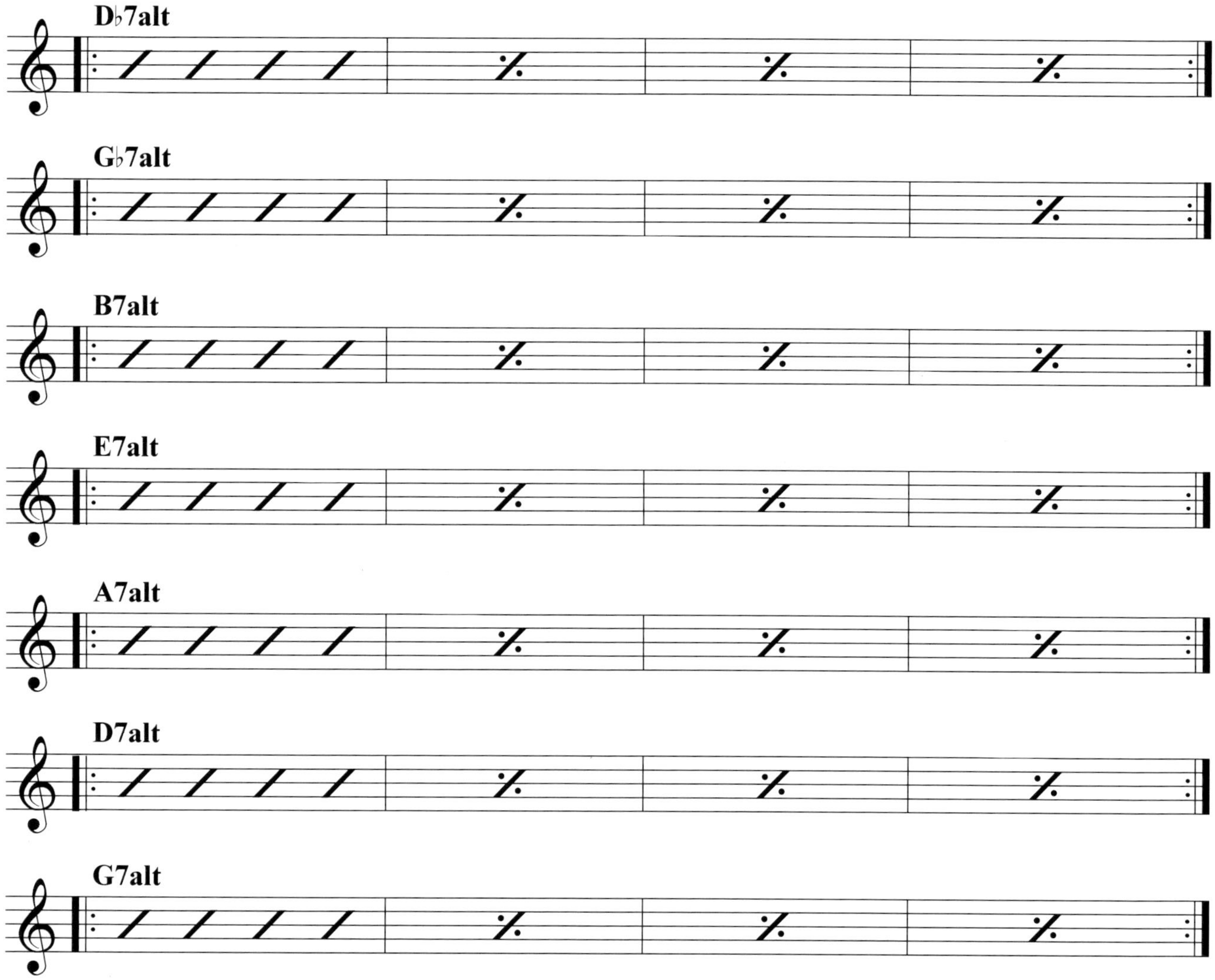

The following exercise shows how the altered scale may be used to solo over altered dominant chords.

CD #21

Bebop Scales

Bebop Scales

David Baker, one of the world's finest jazz educators, named these scales the "bebop scales" because they were used so often by jazz artists from the Bebop Era. These artists included Charlie Christian, Charlie Parker, Lester Young, and Dizzy Gillespie to name a few. Because these artists had crucial roles in developing the jazz language, every serious jazz musician should have a fluent knowledge of these scales. There are three different bebop scales. These are the major bebop, Dorian bebop, and the Mixolydian (or dominant) bebop scales. Each of these scales has eight notes (nine if the octave is counted) rather than seven. The extra note allows the scale to be played, using eighth notes, in exactly four beats (one complete measure of 4/4 time). If the scale is played with a chord tone on a strong beat (downbeat), in the case of the major and Mixolydian bebop scales, all of the other chord tones will be played on the downbeat. Because each of these scales has different function and relates to different chord types, they will be presented one at a time.

Major Bebop

The major bebop scale is a major scale with an extra note between the fifth and sixth steps. It is compared to a major scale below. In the following example, the chord tones of a major chord are shown in the scale. Notice when eighth notes are used, each of the downbeats is a chord tone from a major sixth chord.

C Major **C Major Bebop**

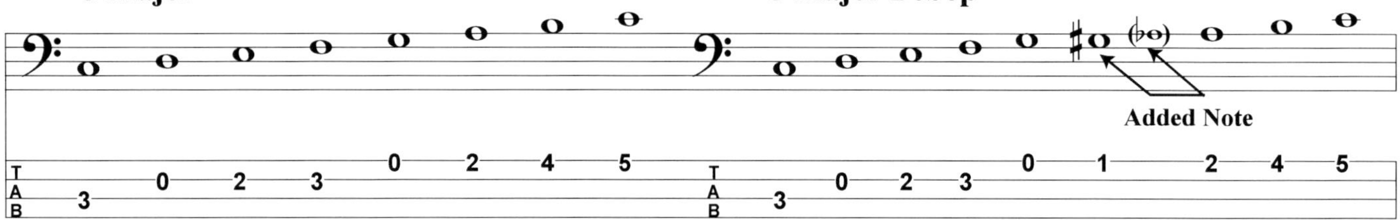

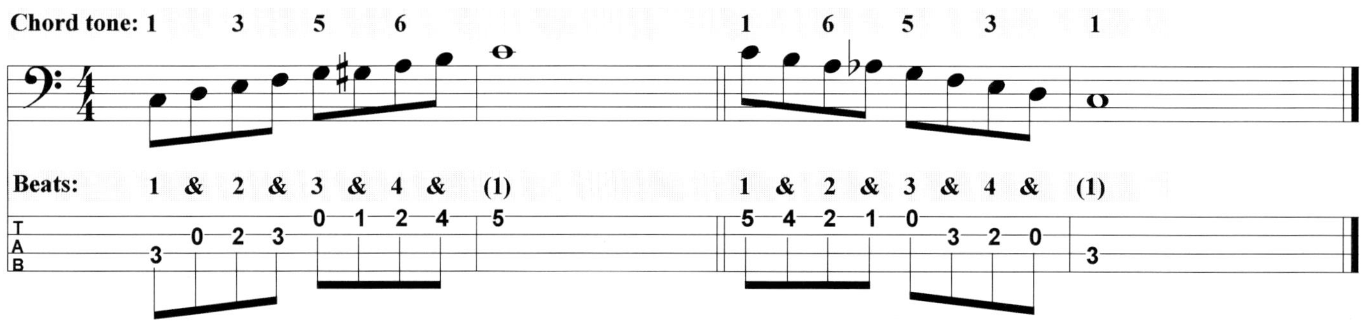

The major bebop's construction shown below with a linear diagram on only the fourth string. Also, one-octave and two-octave patterns are given.

Construction: whole step, whole step, half step, whole step, half step, half step, whole step, half step

F Major Bebop

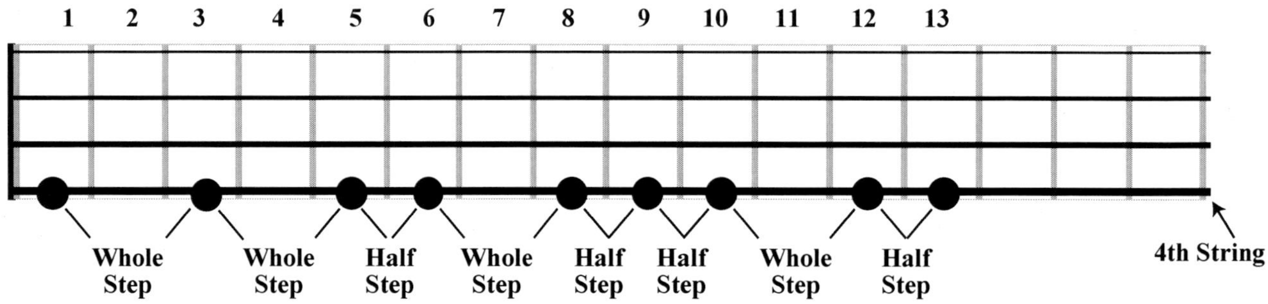

One-Octave Patterns - Major Bebop

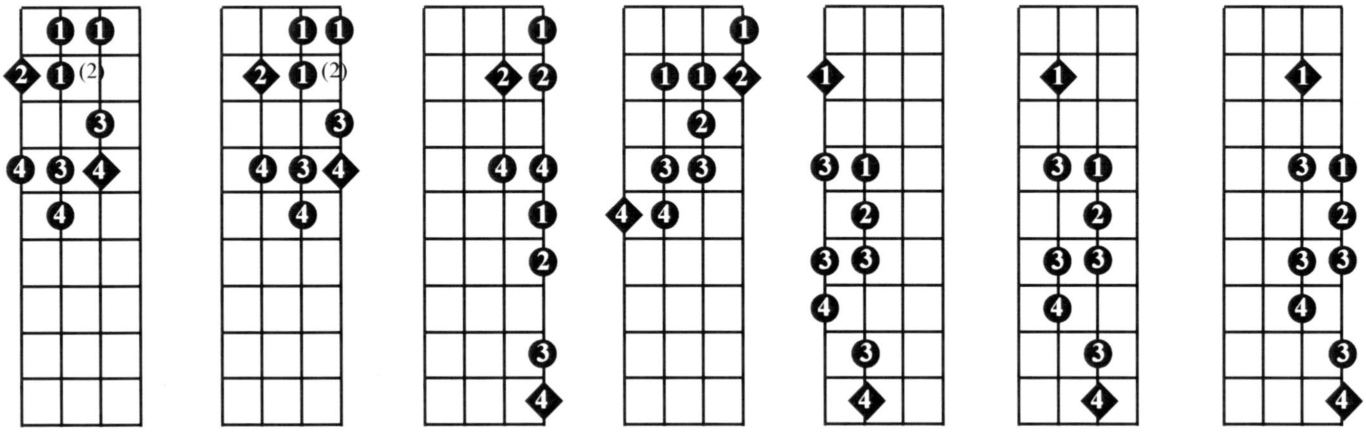

Two-Octave Patterns - Major Bebop

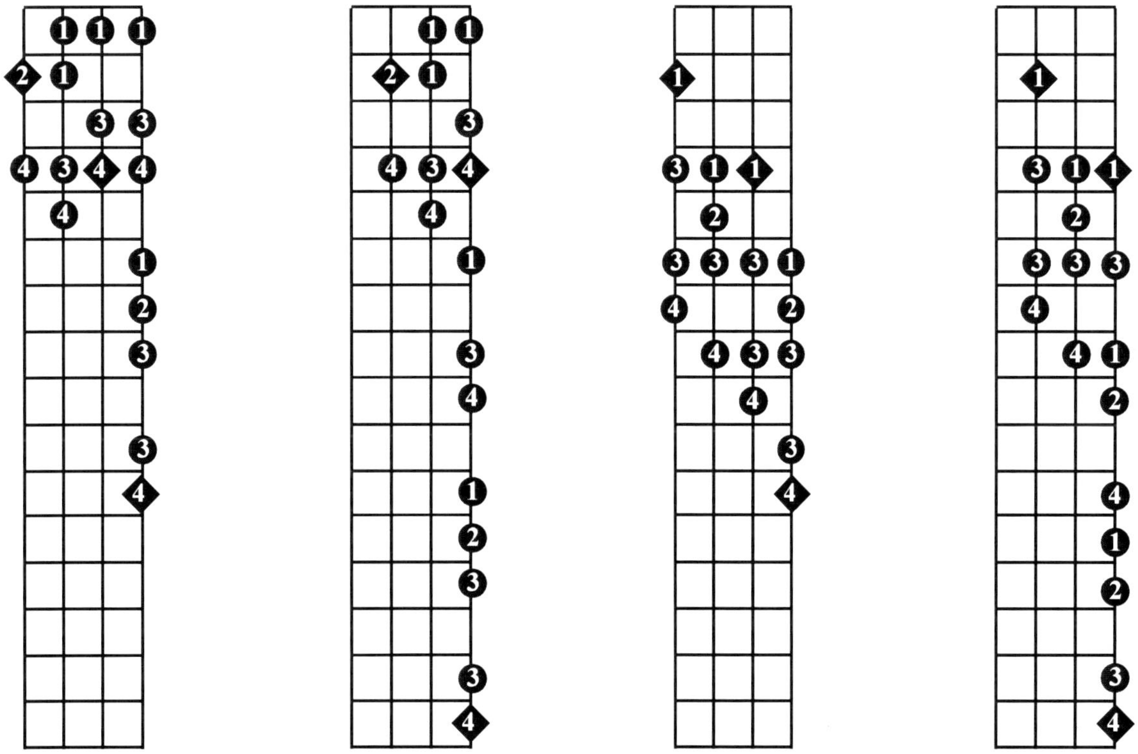

As the name implies, the major bebop scale may be used anywhere a major scale is used. For this reason, the following rhythm track using major sixth chords has been provided. As the student practices this scale with the rhythm track, he/she will be able to hear how the scale relates to the chords. Practice this scale using eighth notes ascending and descending with the chord tones being played on the downbeats.

CD #22 (also try with #2)

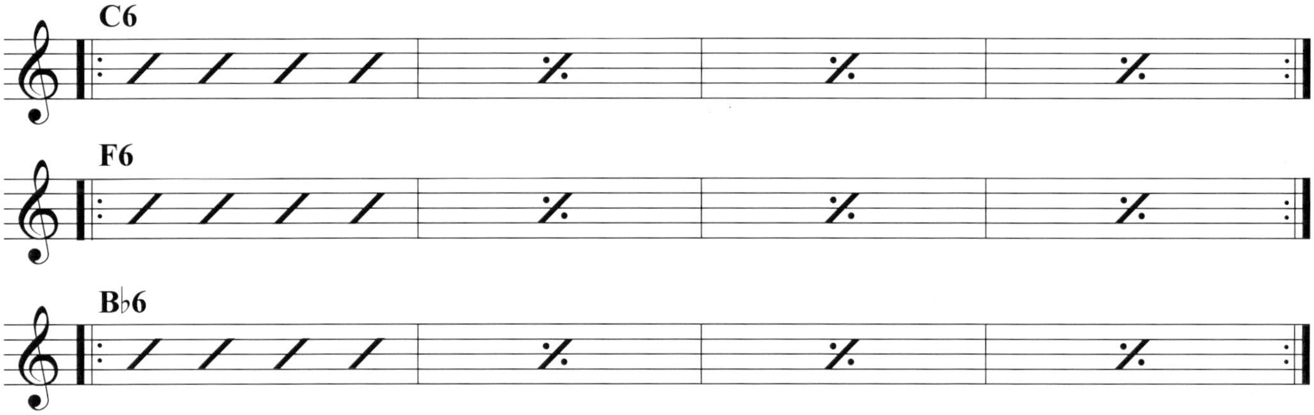

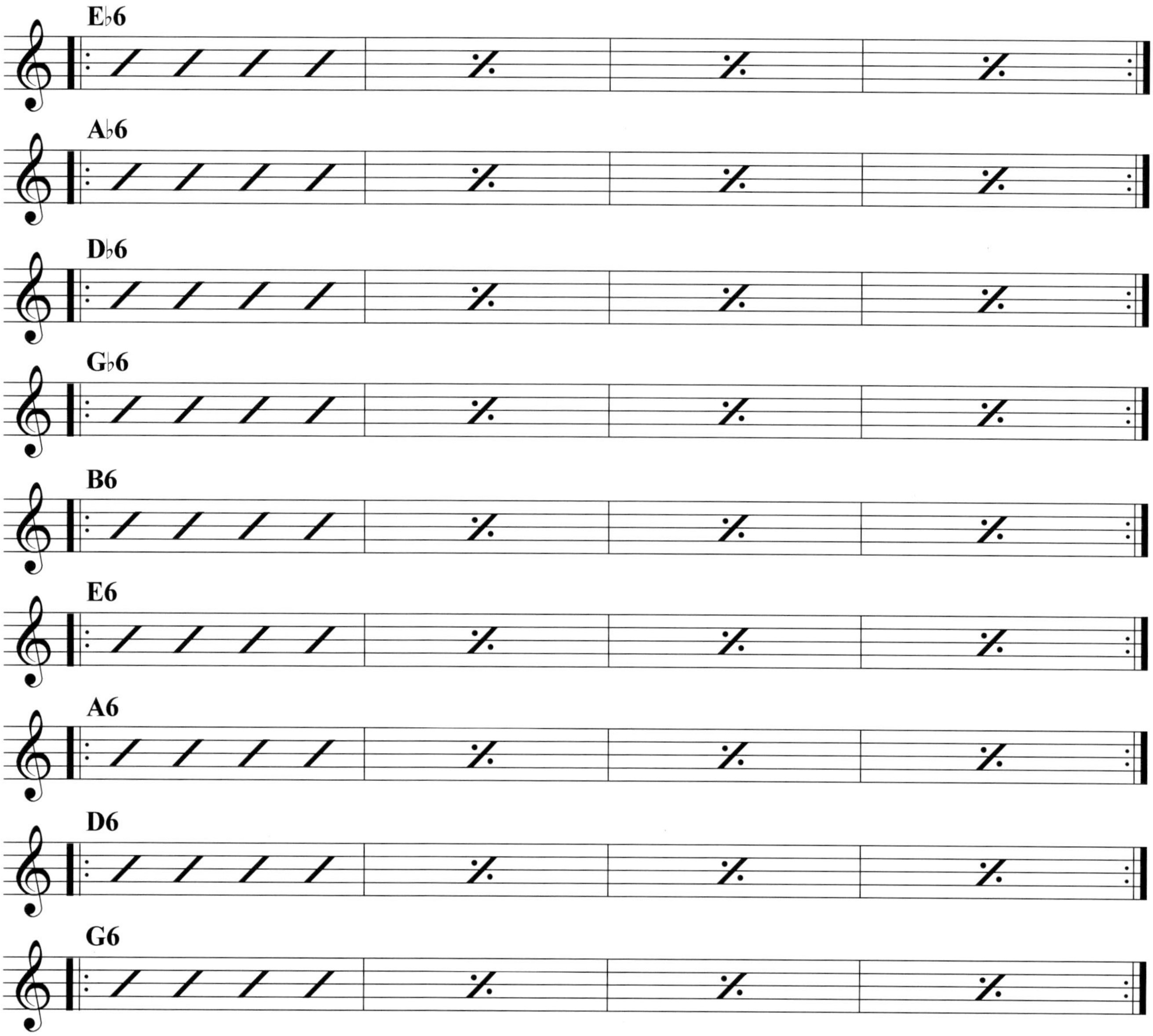

The following exercise demonstrates how the major bebop scale may be used to improvise over major sixth chords.

CD #23

Dorian Bebop

The Dorian bebop scale is the Dorian mode with an extra note between the third and fourth notes. It is compared to the Dorian mode below.

D Dorian **D Dorian Bebop**

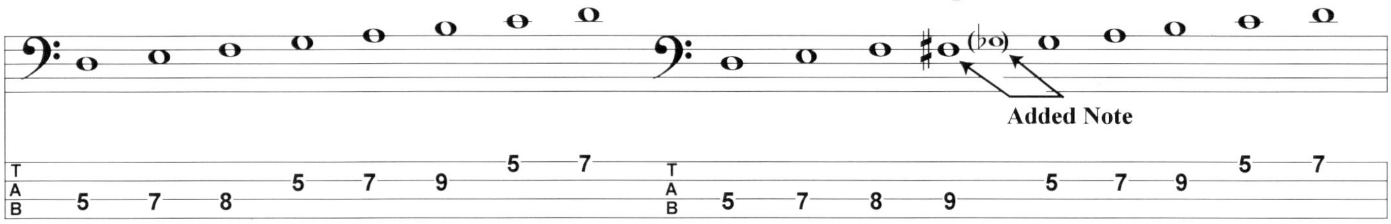

The Dorian bebop's construction is shown below with a linear diagram on only the fourth string. Also, one-octave and two-octave patterns are given.

Construction: whole step, half step, half step, half step, whole step, whole step, half step, whole step

F Dorian Bebop

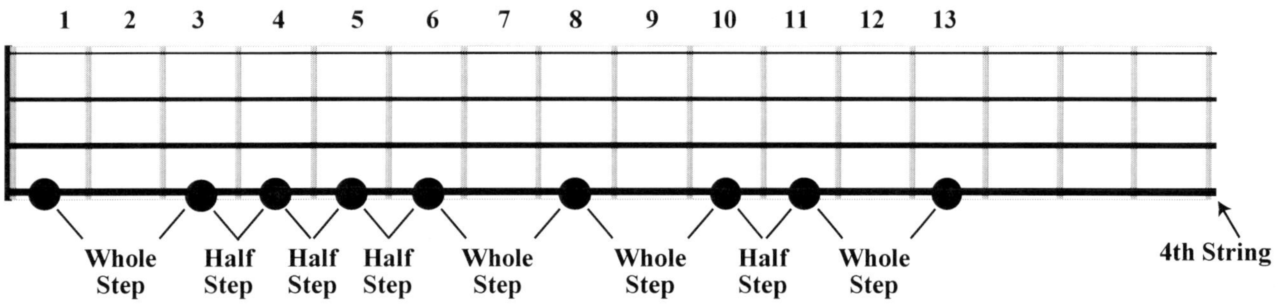

One-Octave Patterns - Dorian Bebop

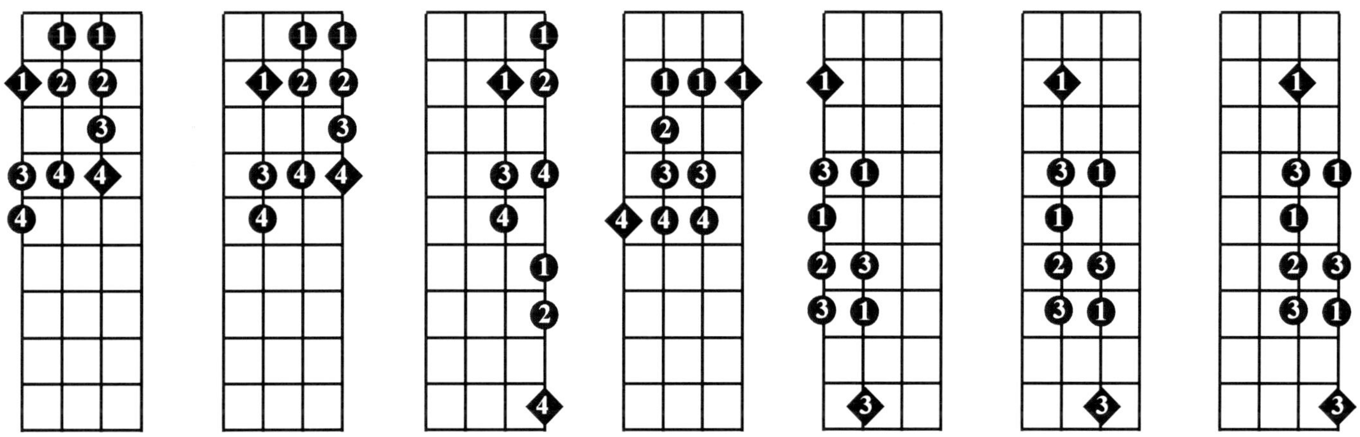

Two-Octave Patterns - Dorian Bebop

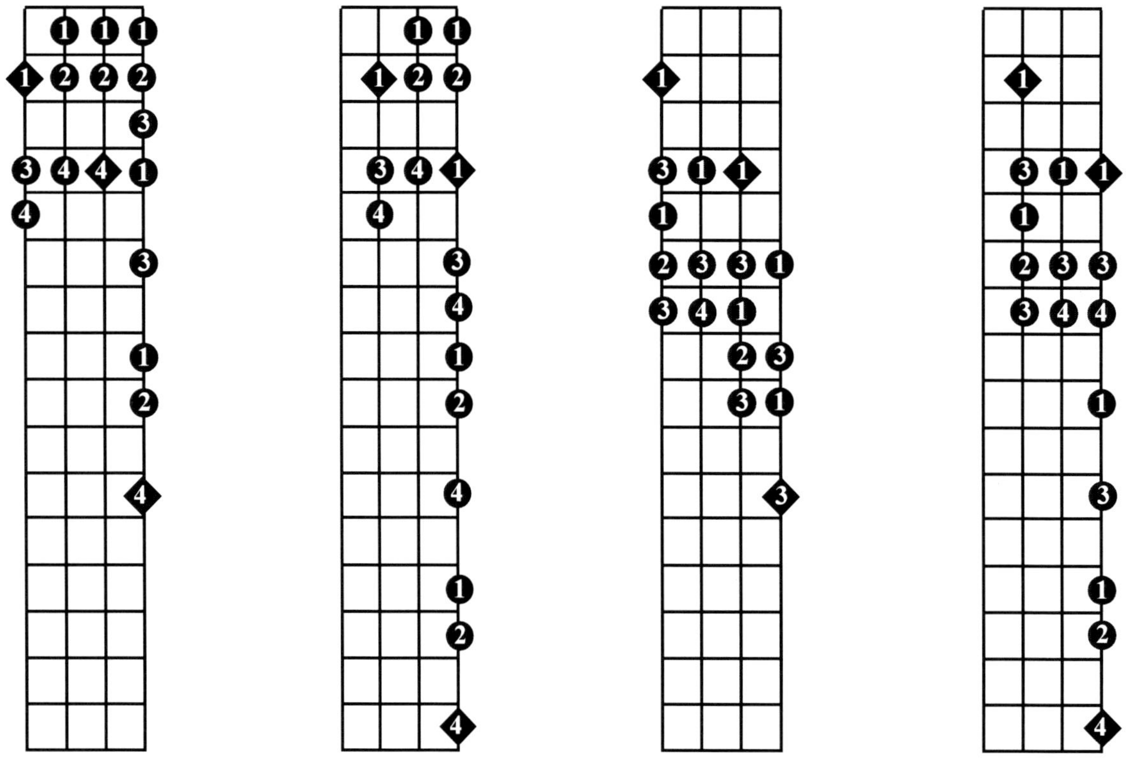

The Dorian bebop scale, like the Dorian mode, may be used against minor seventh chords and minor seventh chord embellishments. The following rhythm track has been provided for practicing the Dorian bebop scale.

CD #4, #7

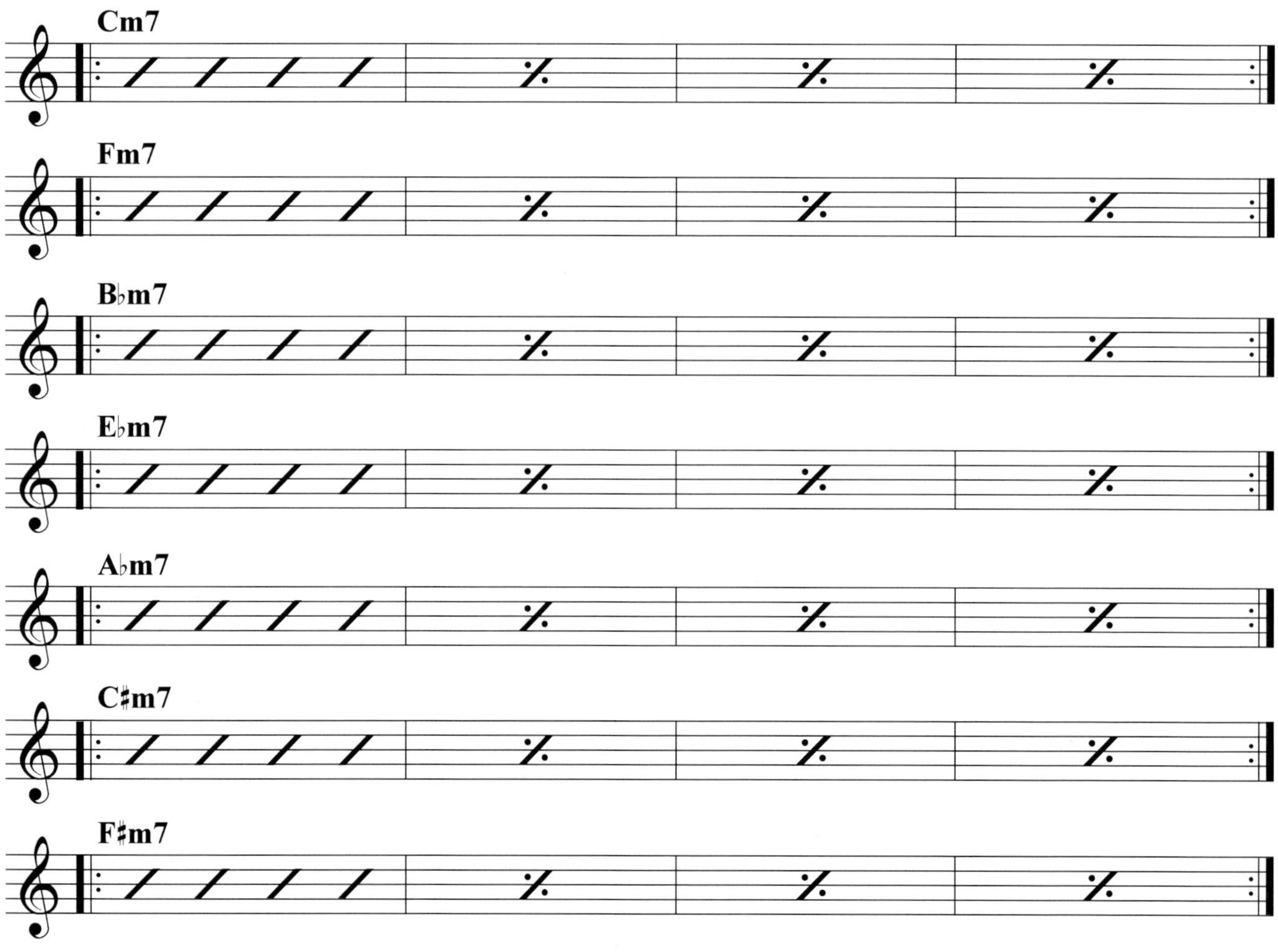

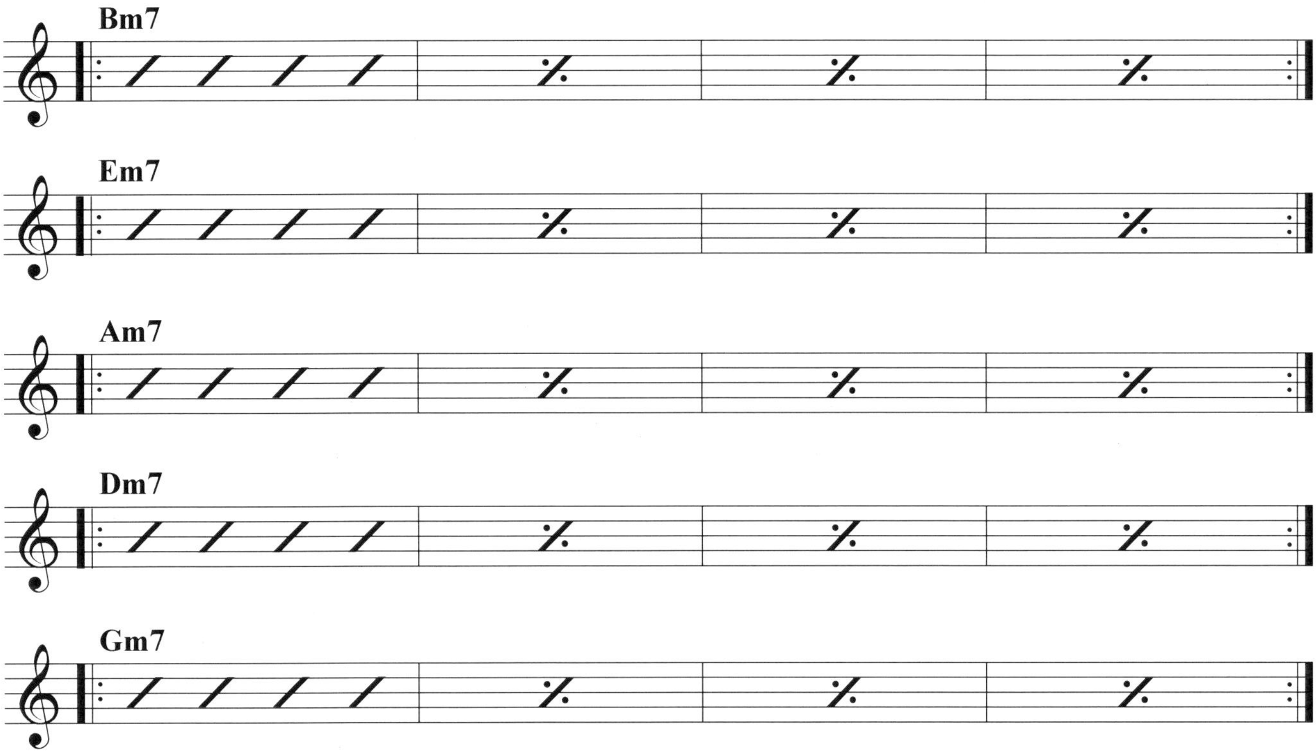

The following exercise demonstrates how the Dorian bebop scale may be used to improvise over minor seventh chords.

CD #24

Mixolydian Bebop

The Mixolydian bebop scale is the same as the Mixolydian mode, but has an extra note located between the seventh step and the root. It is compared to the Mixolydian mode below. The Mixolydian bebop scale has also been written in eighth notes to show how the chord tones of a dominant seventh chord will be played on the downbeats.

G Mixolydian **G Mixolydian Bebop**

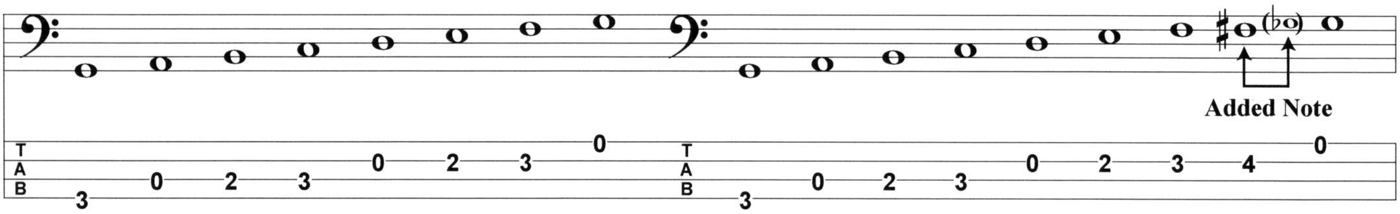

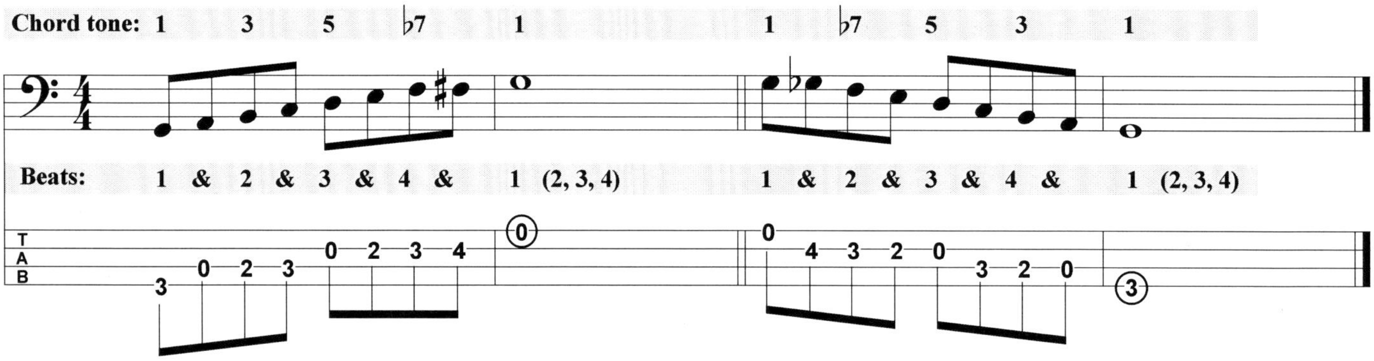

The Mixolydian bebop's construction is shown below with a linear diagram on only the fourth string. Also, one-octave and two-octave patterns are given.

Construction: whole step, whole step, half step, whole step, whole step, half step, half step, half step.

F Mixolydian Bebop

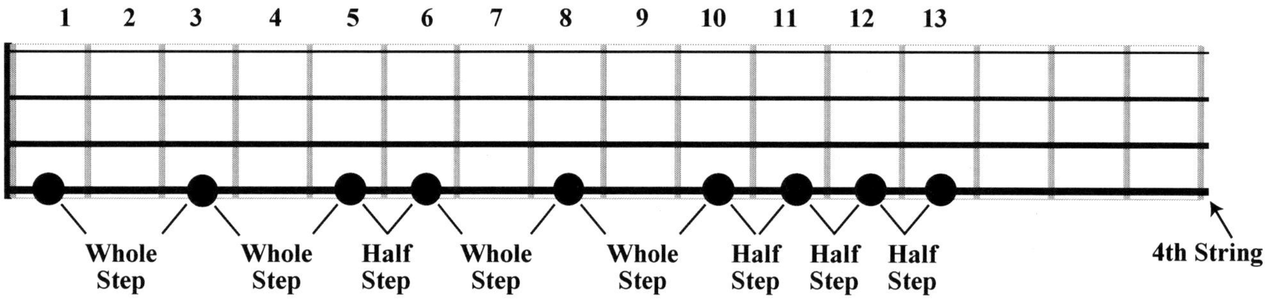

One-Octave Patterns - Mixolydian Bebop

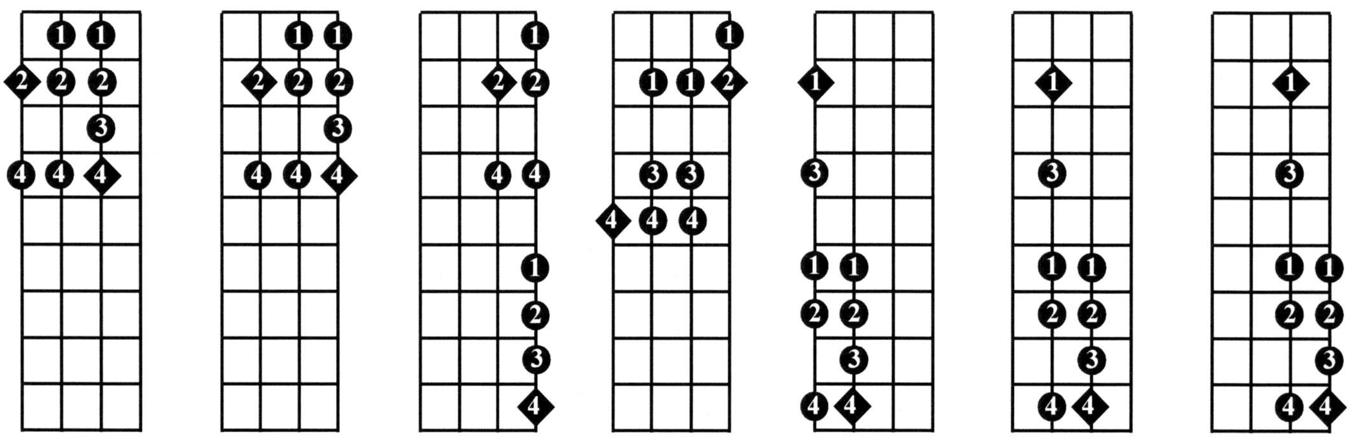

Two-Octave Patterns - Mixolydian Bebop

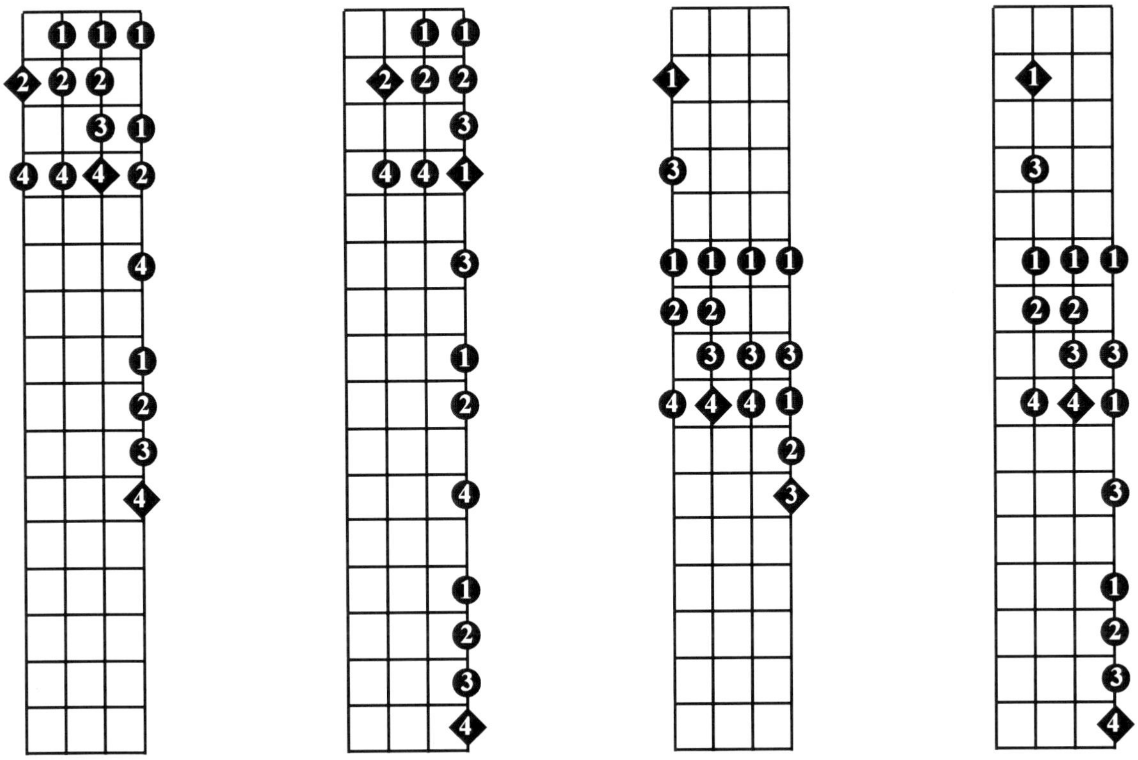

Like the Mixolydian mode, the Mixolydian bebop scale may be used against dominant seventh chords. The following rhythm track will allow the student to hear how this scales relates to dominant seventh chords while the scale is being practiced and learned.

CD #11

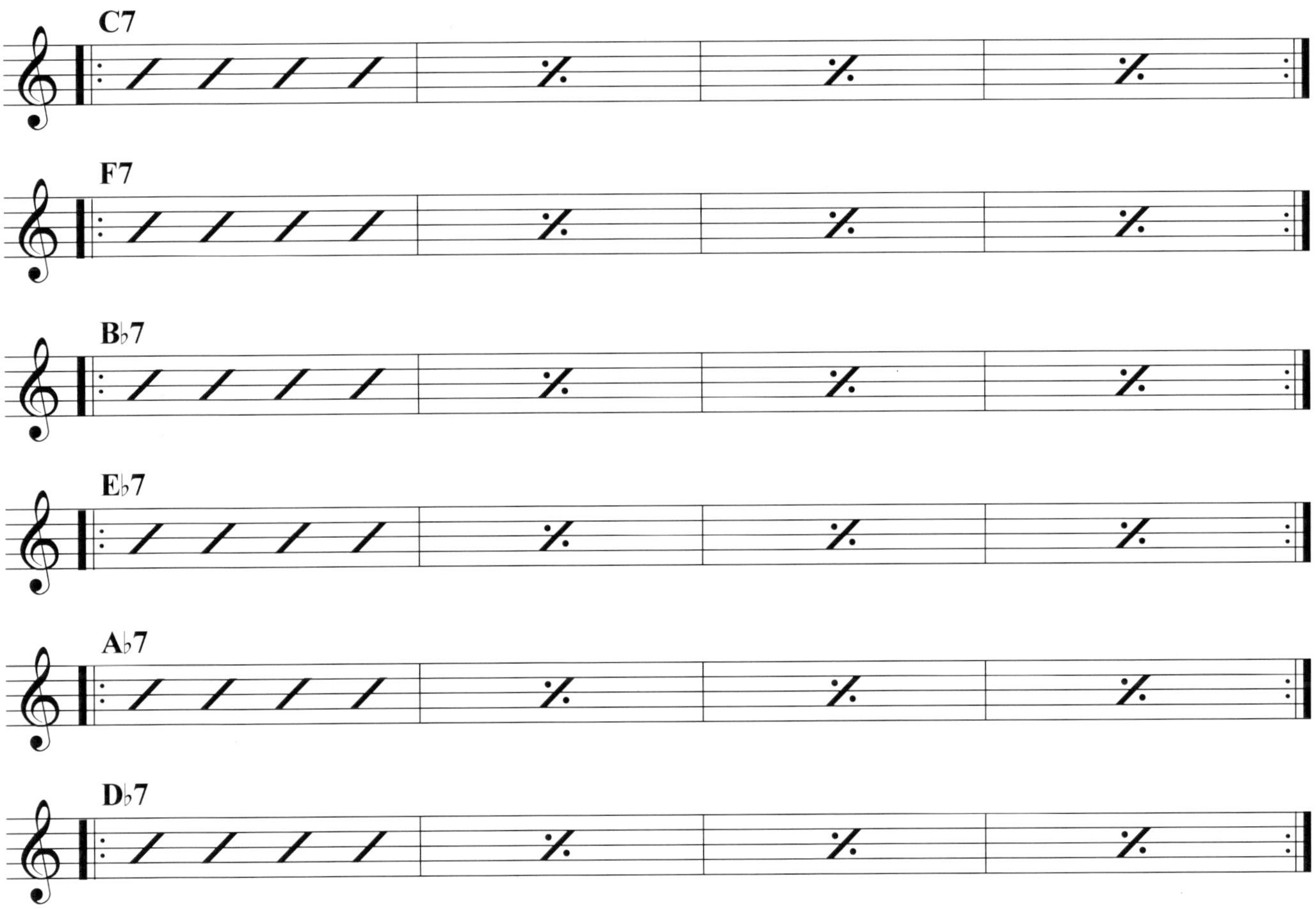

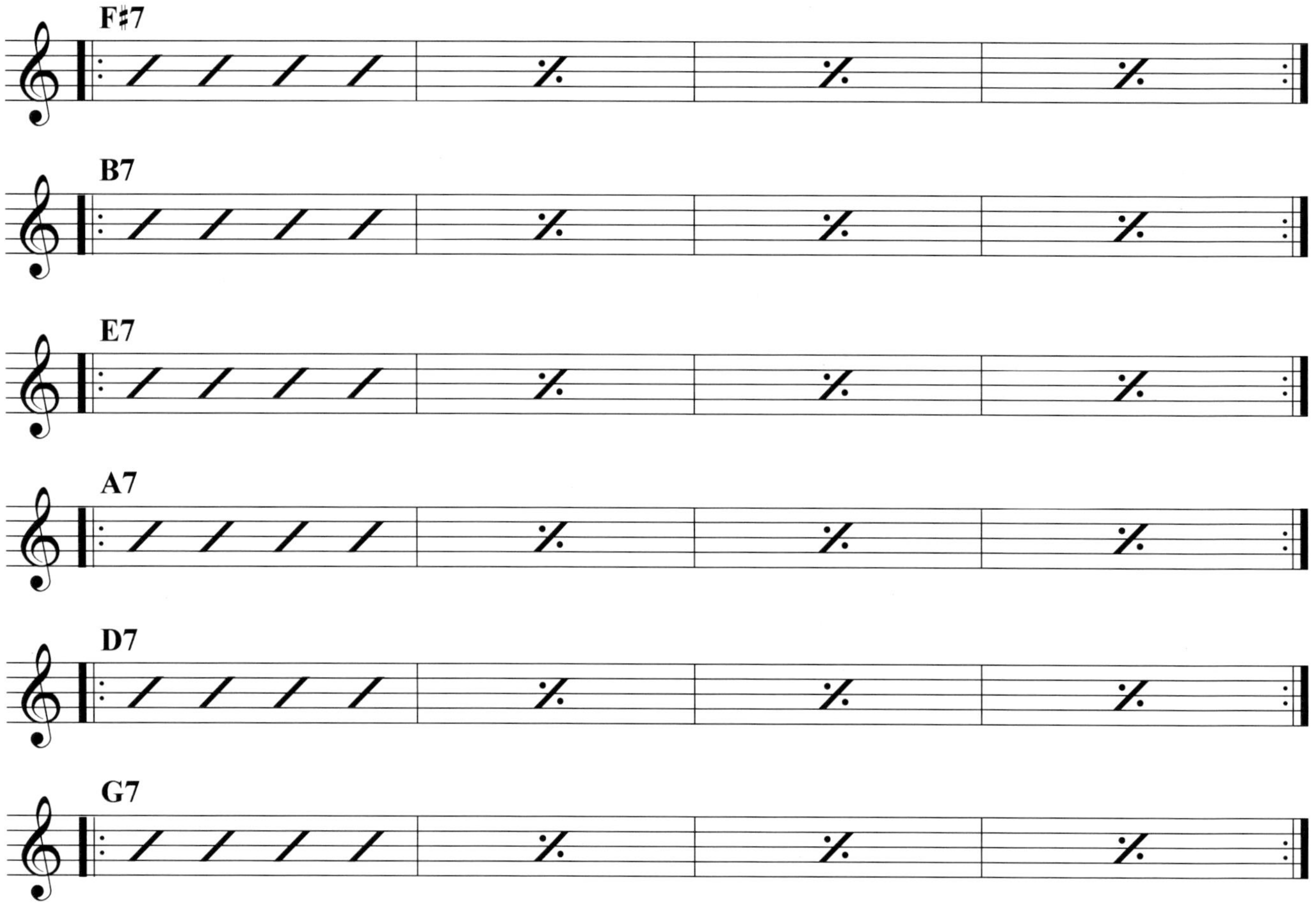

The following exercise demonstrates how the Mixolydian bebop scale can be used to improvise over dominant seventh chords.

CD #25

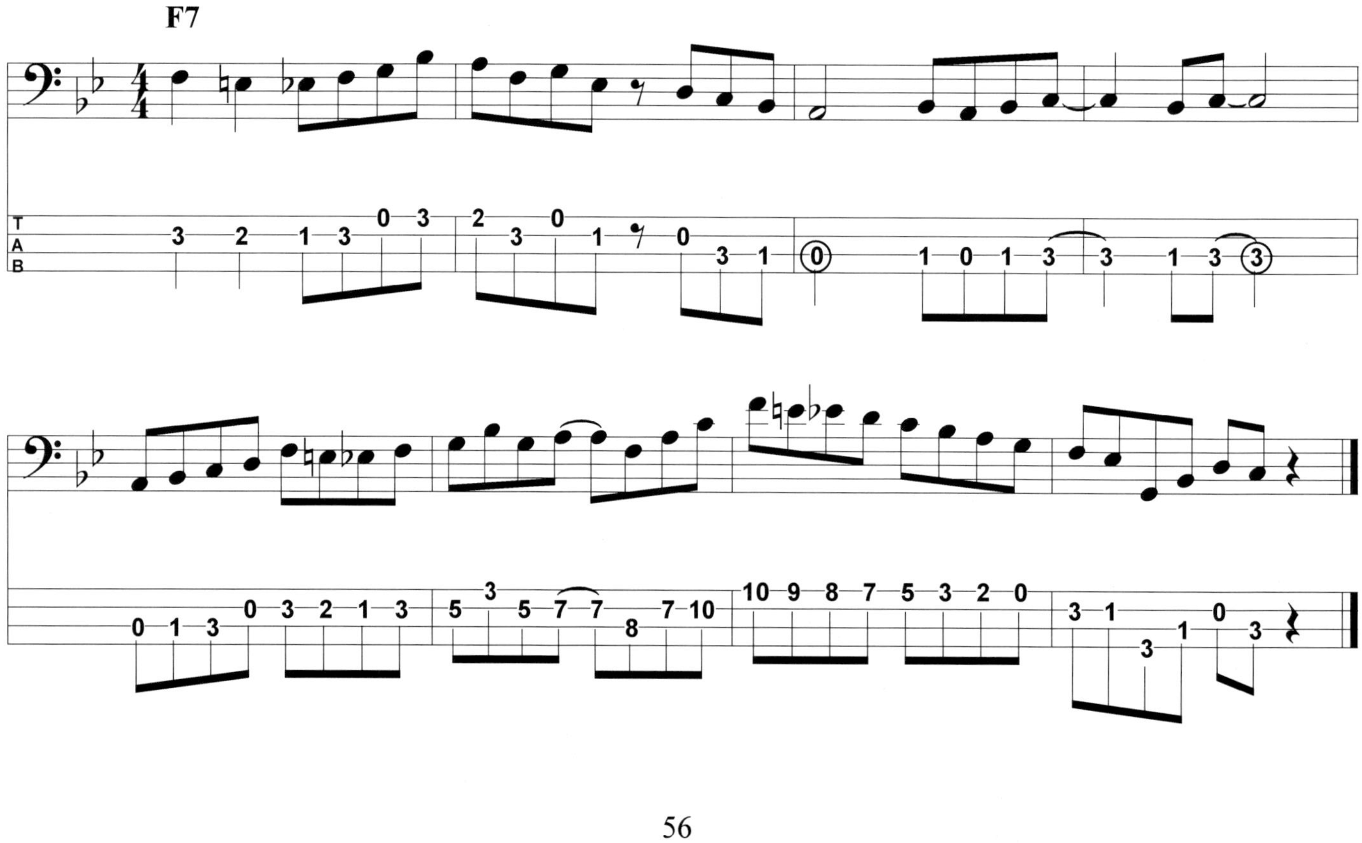

Pentatonic Scales

Pentatonic Scales

Pentatonic scales, as the name implies, are five-note scales. The two pentatonic scales that will be covered are the major and minor pentatonic.

Major Pentatonic

The major pentatonic scale is a major scale without any half steps. The fourth and the seventh steps have been removed. This can be seen by comparing the major pentatonic to the major scale below.

C Major **C Major Pentatonic**

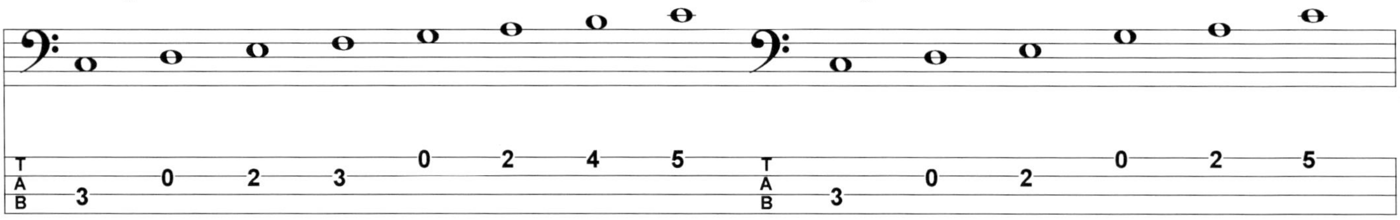

The major pentatonic scale's construction is shown below. A linear diagram of this scale with the root on the fourth string has also been provided. One-octave and two-octave patterns should be practiced to the point of mastery using the major chord rhythm track.

Construction: whole step, whole step, one and a half steps, whole step, one and half steps

F Major Pentatonic

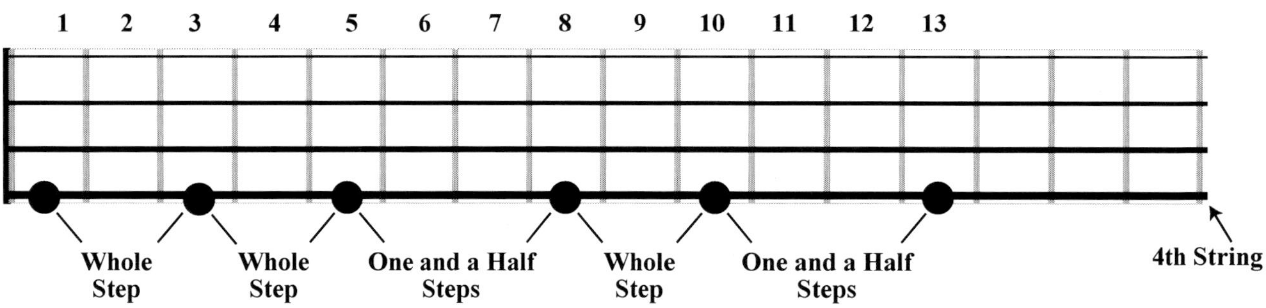

One-Octave Patterns - Major Pentatonic

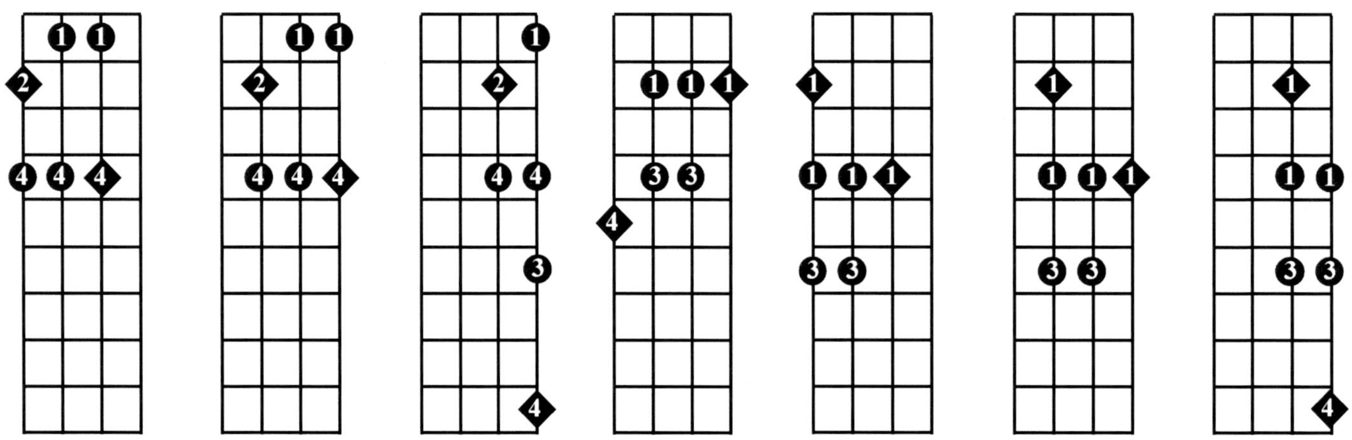

Two-Octave Patterns - Major Pentatonic

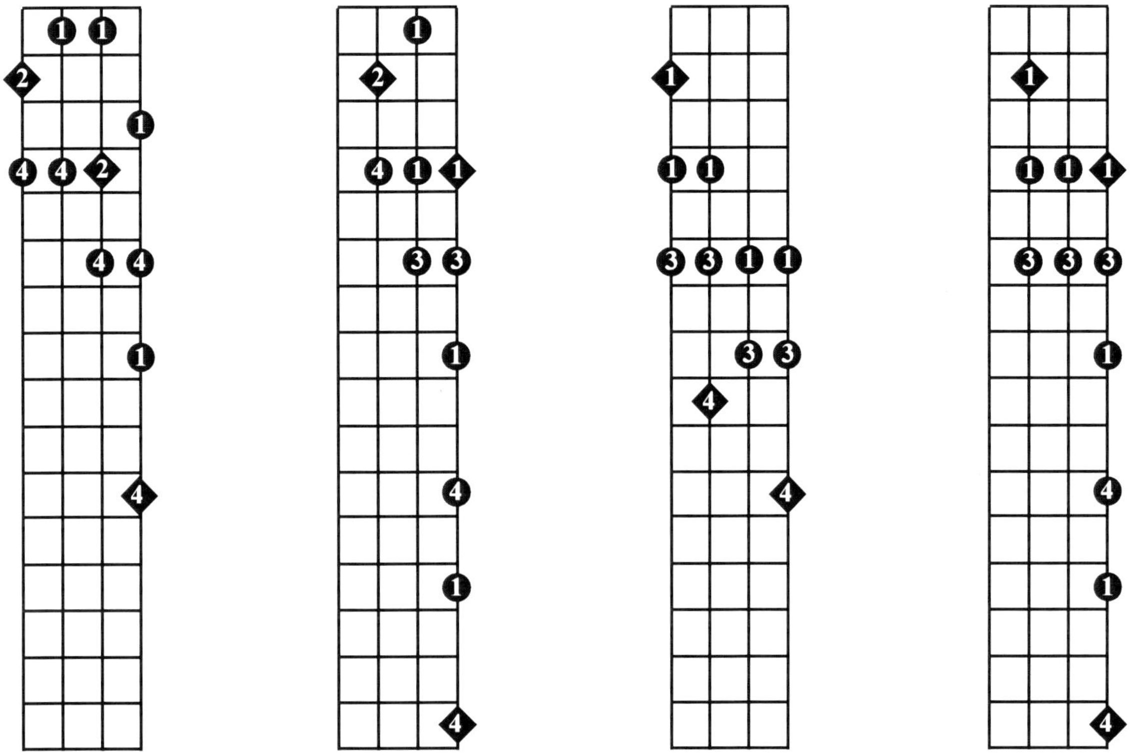

CD #2 (also try with #9 and #22)

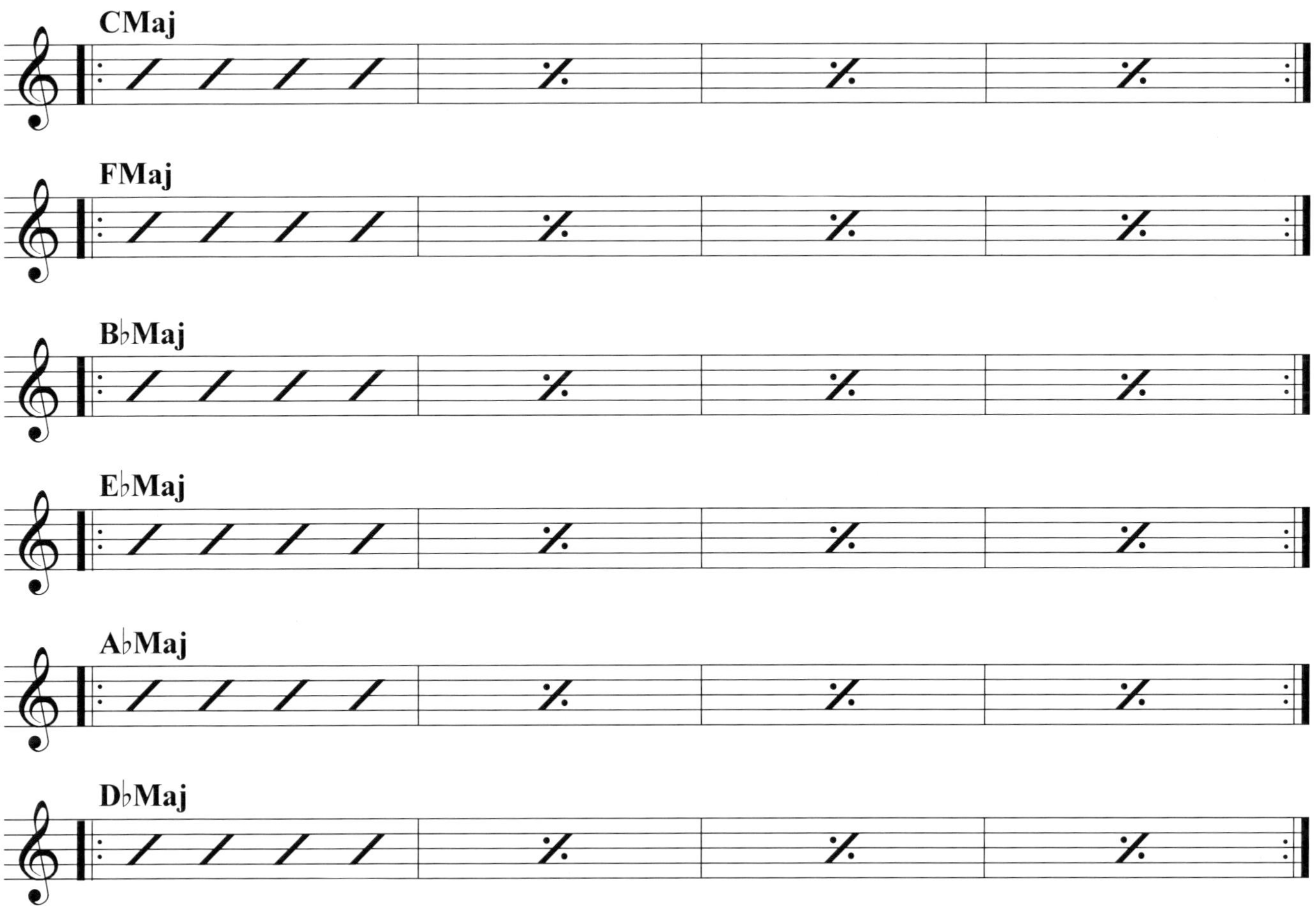

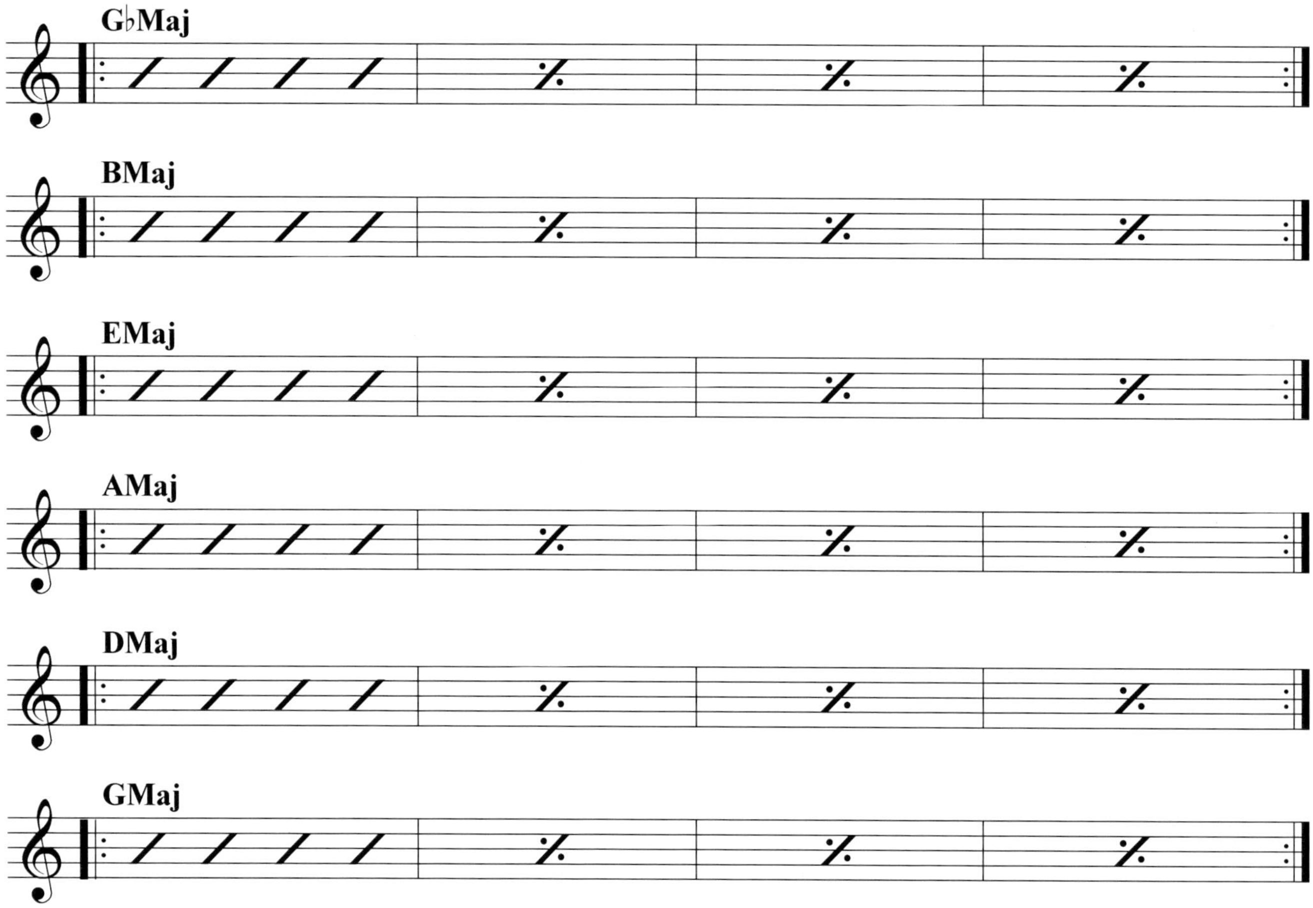

The following exercise demonstrates the use of the major pentatonic scale in jazz improvisation.

CD #26

Minor Pentatonic

The minor pentatonic scale is natural minor scale with the half steps removed. As shown below, the minor pentatonic scale contains the same notes as the natural minor scale, but the second and sixth steps have been omitted.

A Natural Minor **A Minor Pentatonic**

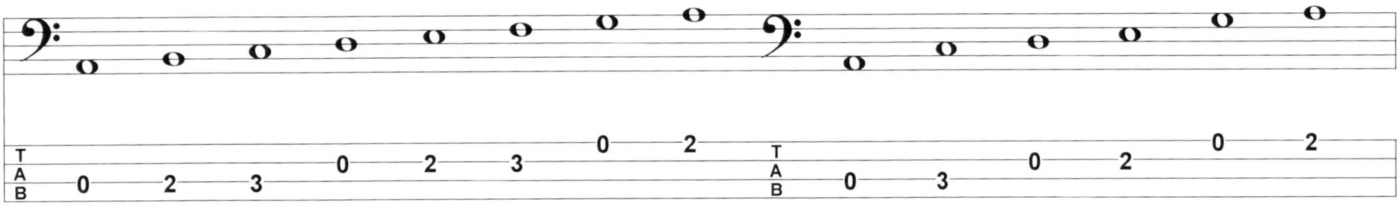

Whole step and half step construction for the minor pentatonic scale is given below. A linear diagram with the root on the fourth string is also given. One-octave and two-octave finger patterns should be practiced with the rhythm tracks provided. Because the minor pentatonic scale is closely related to a natural minor scale, it may be used against minor chords the same way a natural minor scale is used.

Construction: one and half steps, whole step, whole step, one and a half steps, whole step

F Minor Pentatonic

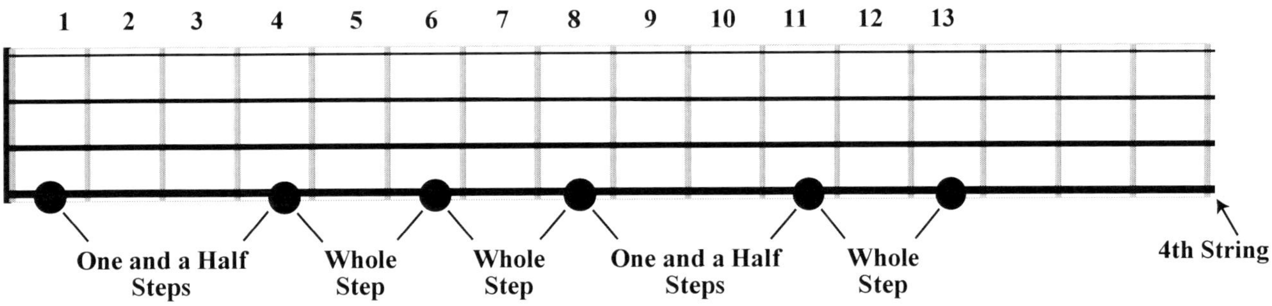

One-Octave Patterns - Minor Pentatonic

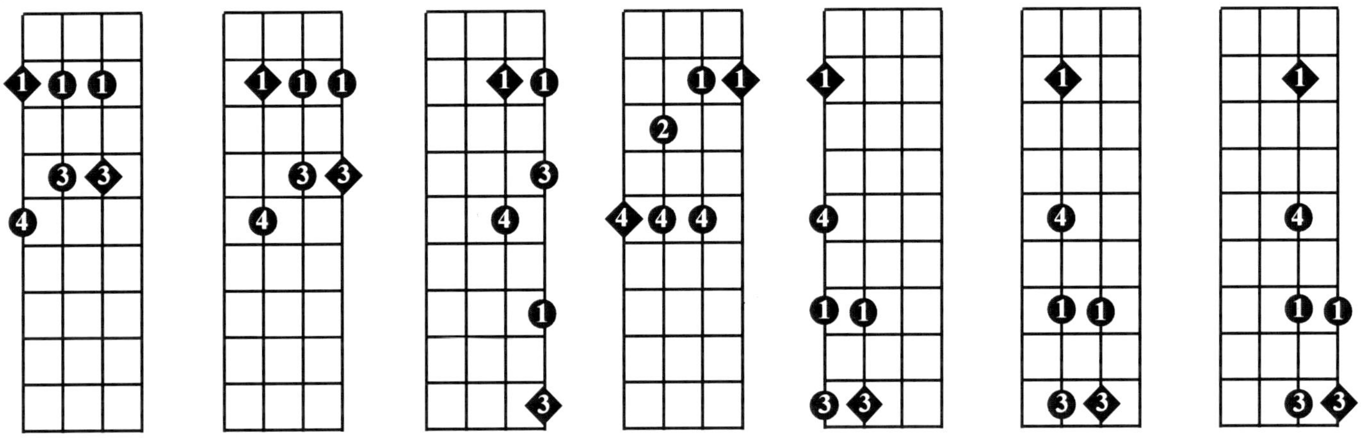

Two-Octave Patterns - Minor Pentatonic

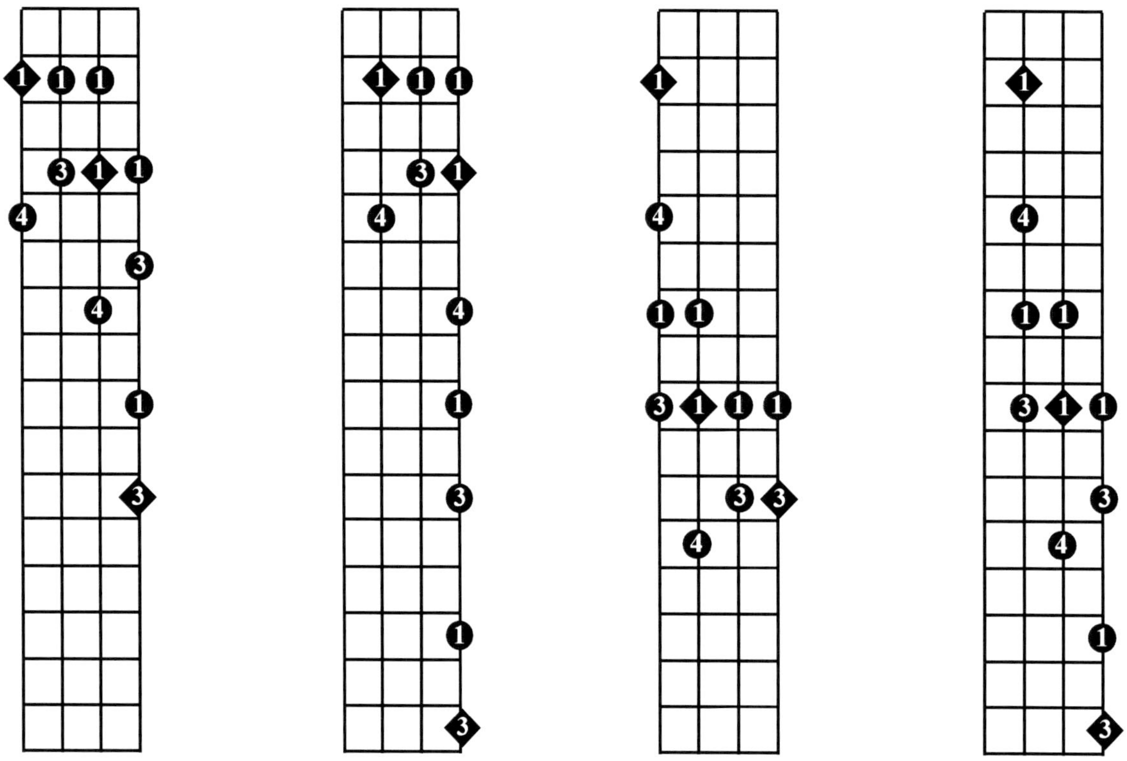

CD #4, #7

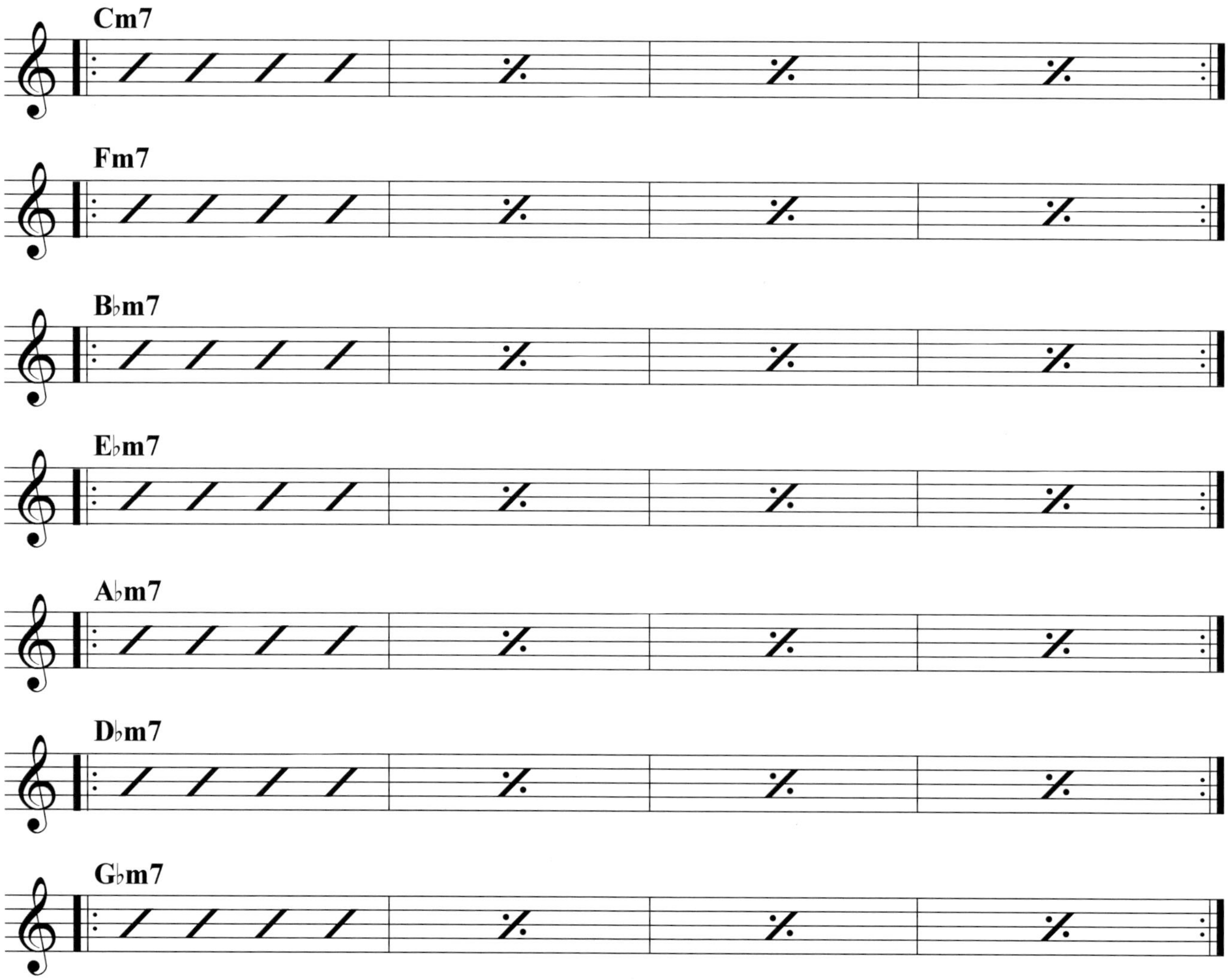

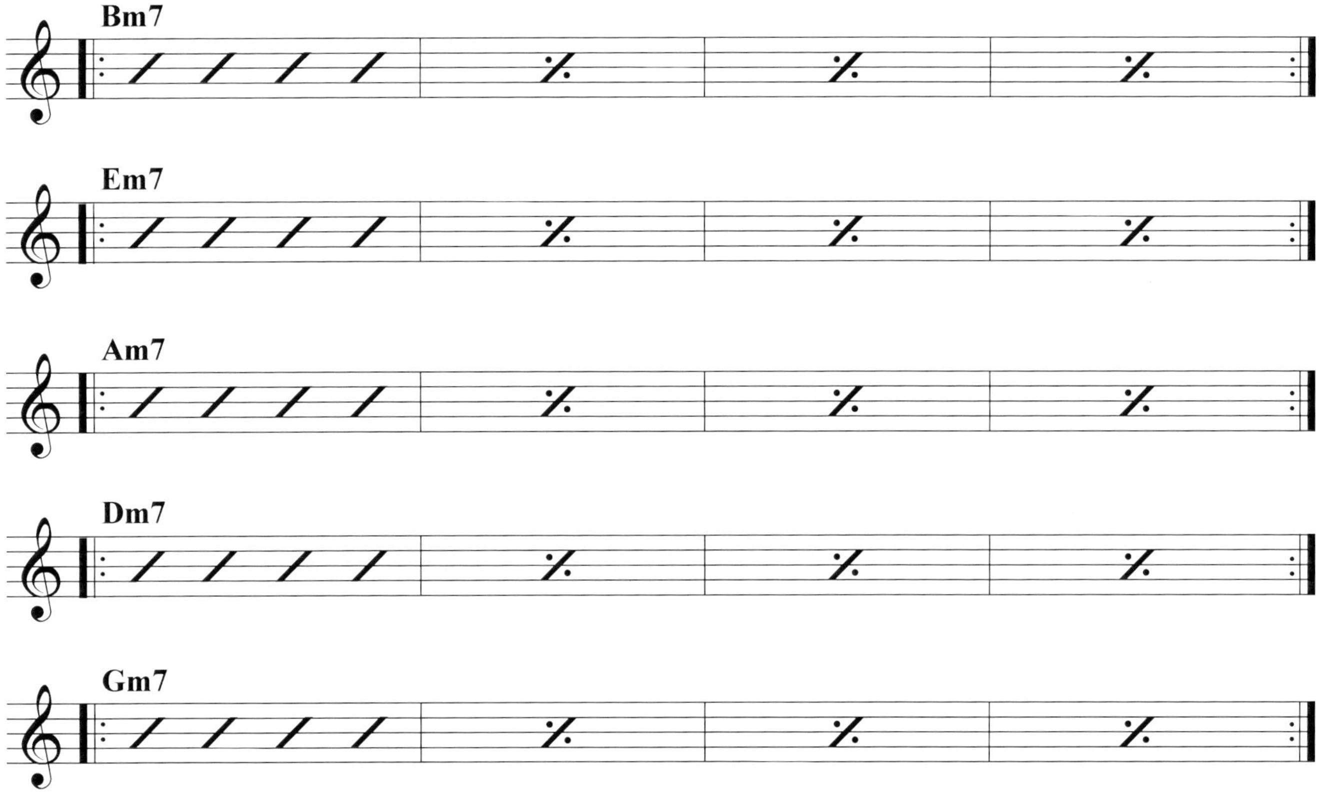

The following exercise demonstrates the use of the minor pentatonic scale.

CD #27

Blues Scales

Blues Scales

The blues scale is a minor pentatonic scale with an added flat five-interval. It is compared to the minor pentatonic scale below.

A Minor Pentatonic **A Blues Scale**

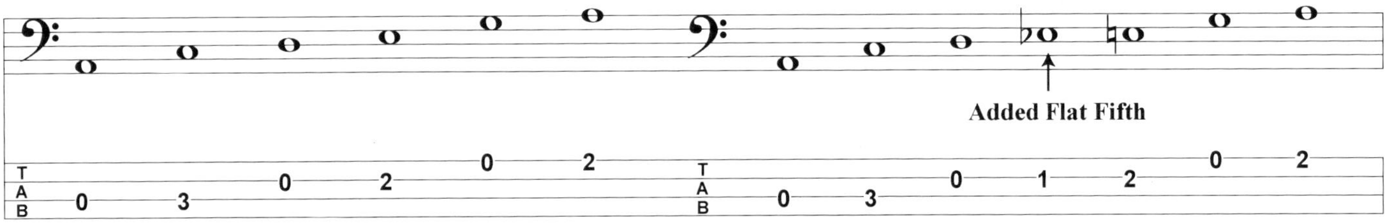

The blues scale's construction, linear diagram on the fourth string, and one-octave and two-octave patterns are shown below.

Construction: one and a half steps, whole step, half step, half step, one and a half steps, whole step

F Blues Scale

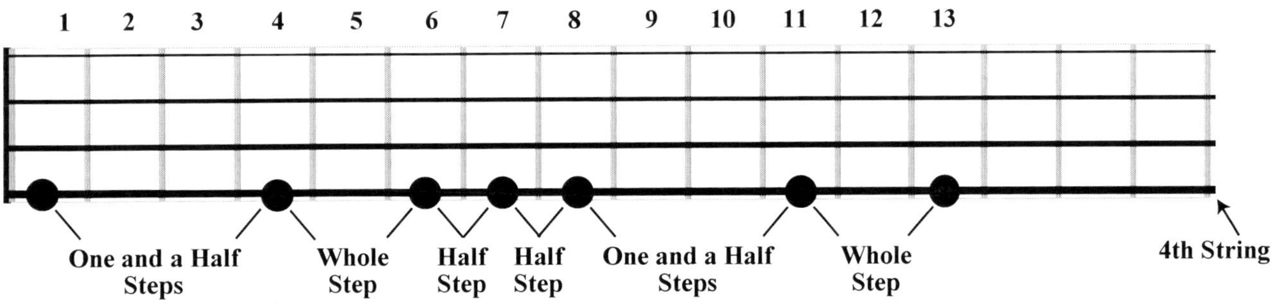

One-Octave Patterns - Blues Scales

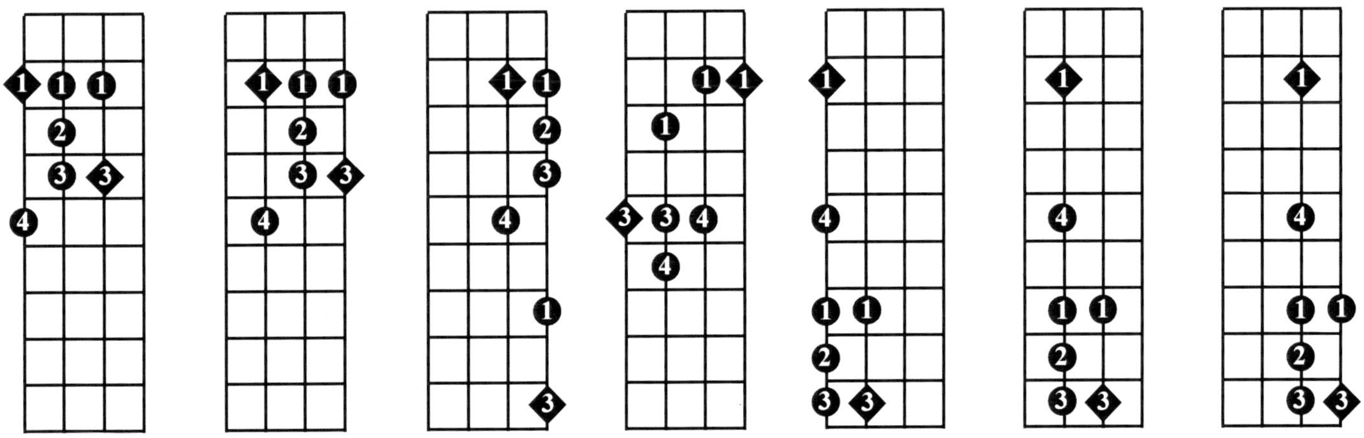

Two-Octave Patterns - Blues Scales

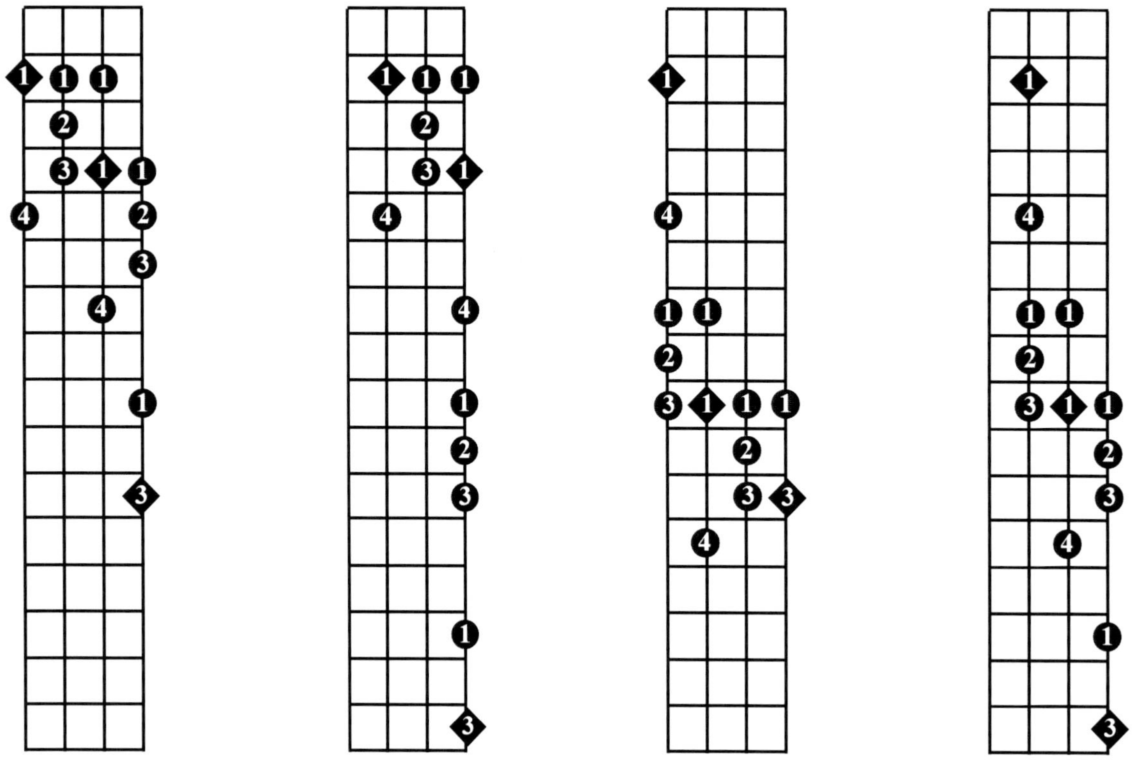

The blues scale works against many different chords including dominant seventh and dominant seventh embellishments, minor seventh and minor seventh embellishments, and sometimes major type chords. Because of this scale's earthy quality, it can give a hint of the blues to almost any chord. To make practicing easier, only dominant seventh chords are provided as a rhythm track for this scale. Make sure to explore many uses for this scale.

CD #11 (also try with #4, #7, #18 and #20)

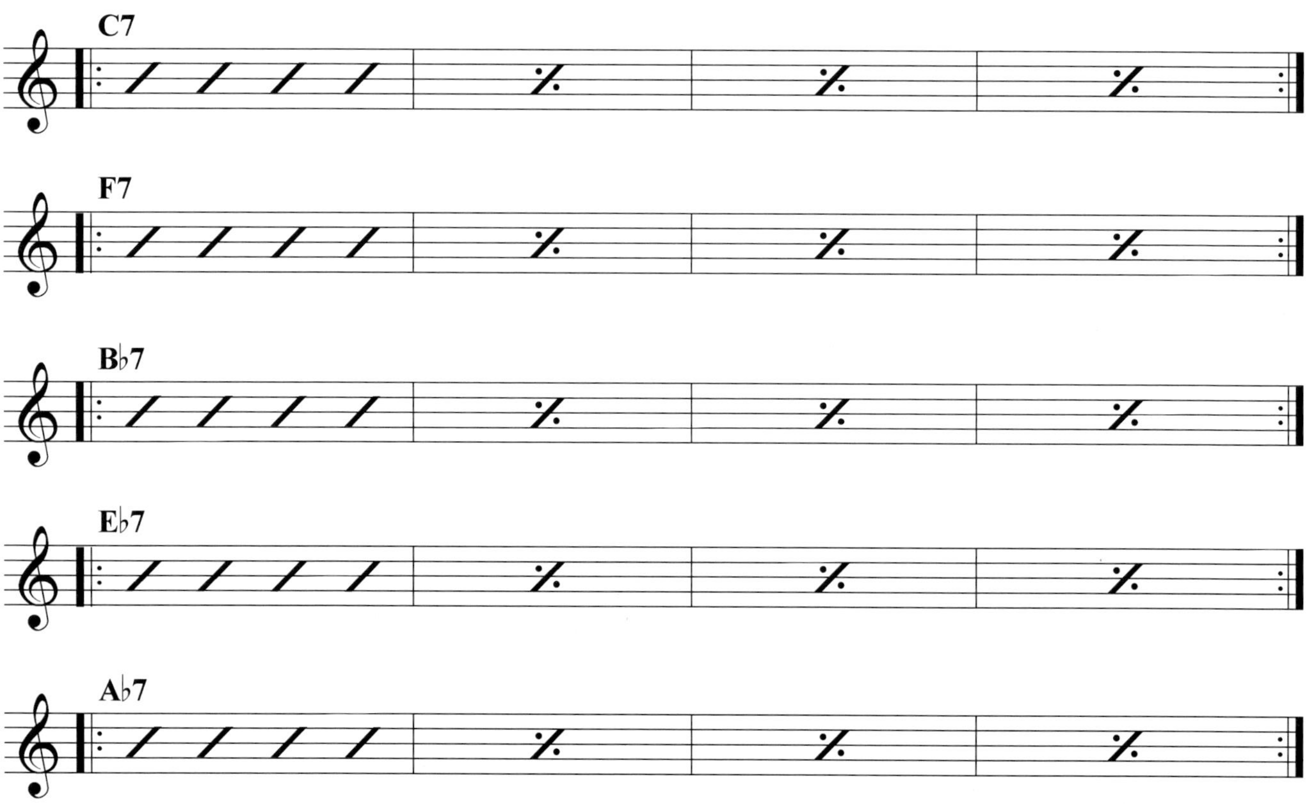

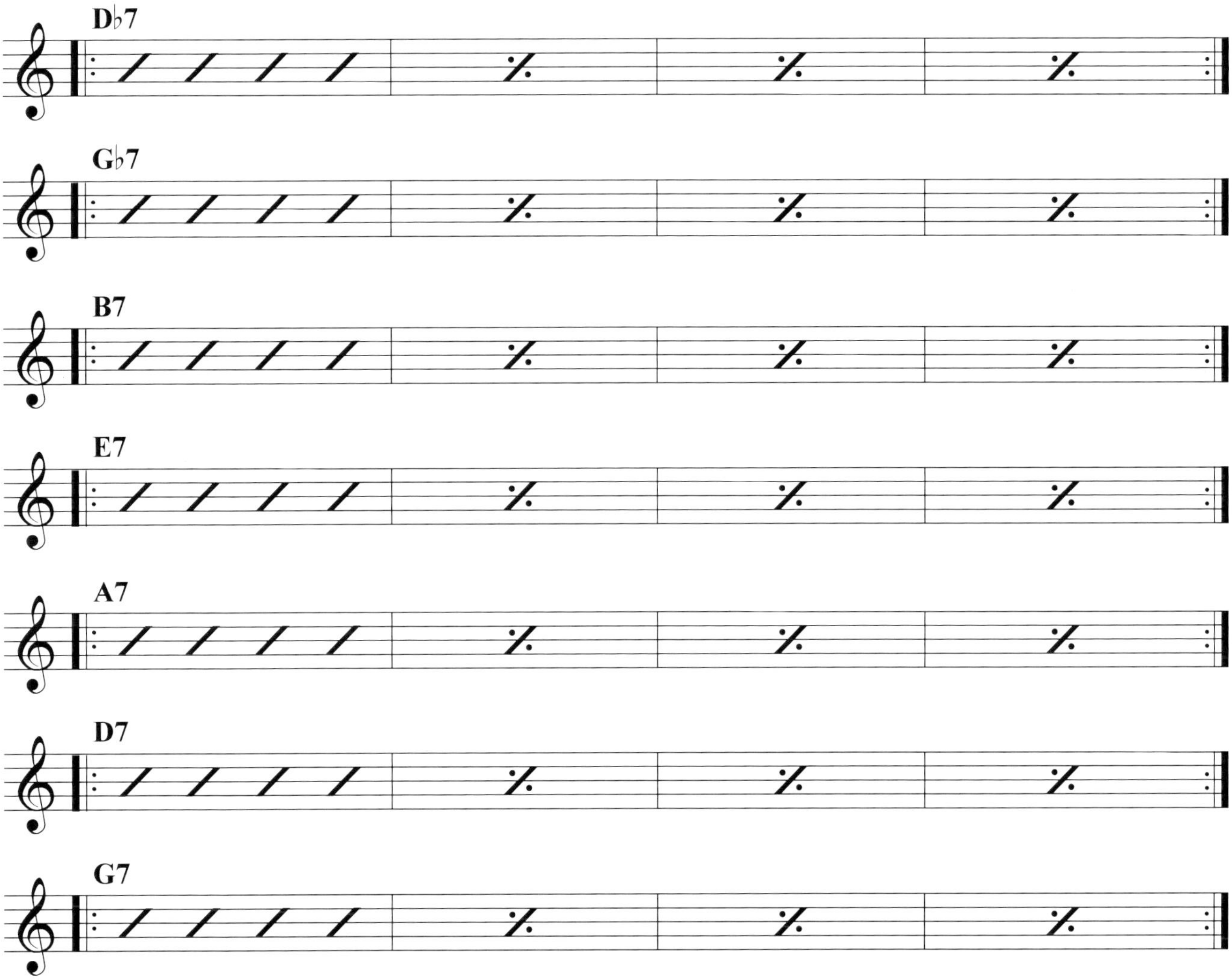

The following exercise makes use of the B♭ blues scale. Even though this scale is closely related to the minor pentatonic scale, it is applied over a dominant seventh chord in this example.

CD #28

Symmetrical Scales

Diminished Scales

The diminished scale is a symmetrical scale. Its construction is made of alternating whole steps and half steps. This construction yields two different applications for this scale. Also, every other note of the scale may be considered the root. This scale will produce the same notes when played one and a half steps (three frets) higher or lower. Both diminished scales will be covered separately.

Diminished Whole-Half

The diminished (whole-half) scale is shown below.

C Diminished (Whole-Half) **G Diminished (Whole-Half)**

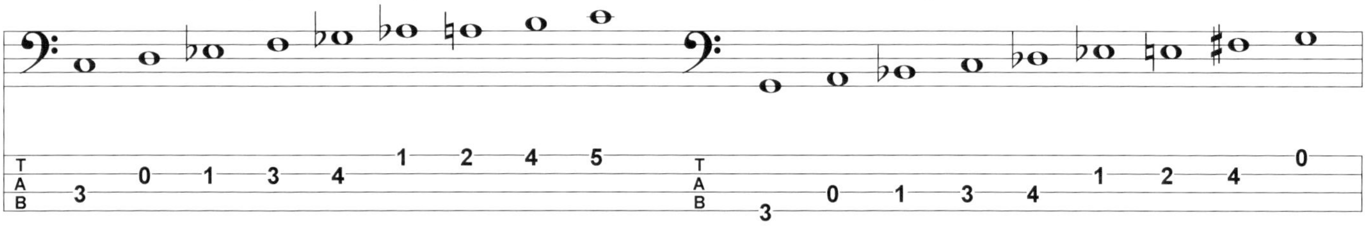

The intervallic construction and a linear diagram of this scale with the root on the fourth string are shown below. One-octave and two-octave patterns have also been provided. As was mentioned earlier, the construction of diminished scales is symmetrical. In the case of the diminished scale, the construction in whole steps and half steps is repeated every other note. The C, E♭, G♭, and A diminished scales contain all of the same notes. Theoretically, there are only three diminished scales. They are: C, C♯, and D. All of the other tonal centers for this scale contain the same notes as the C, C♯, and D diminished scales.

Construction: whole step, half step, whole step, half step, whole step, half step, whole step, half step

F Diminished (Whole-Half)

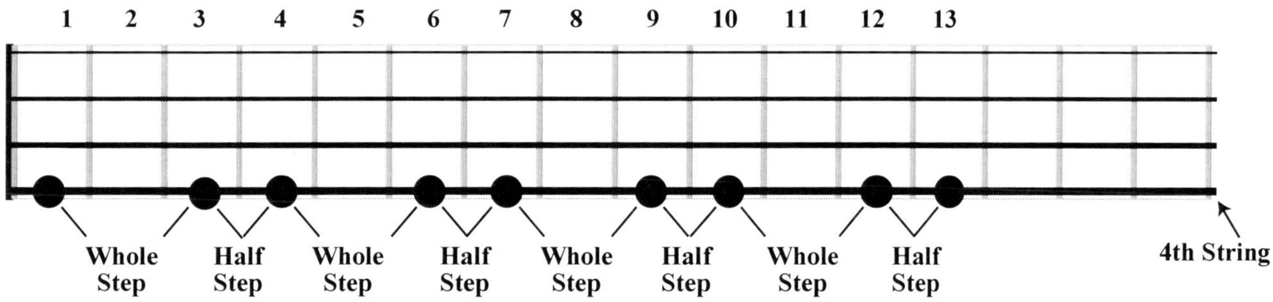

One-Octave Patterns - Diminished (Whole-Half)

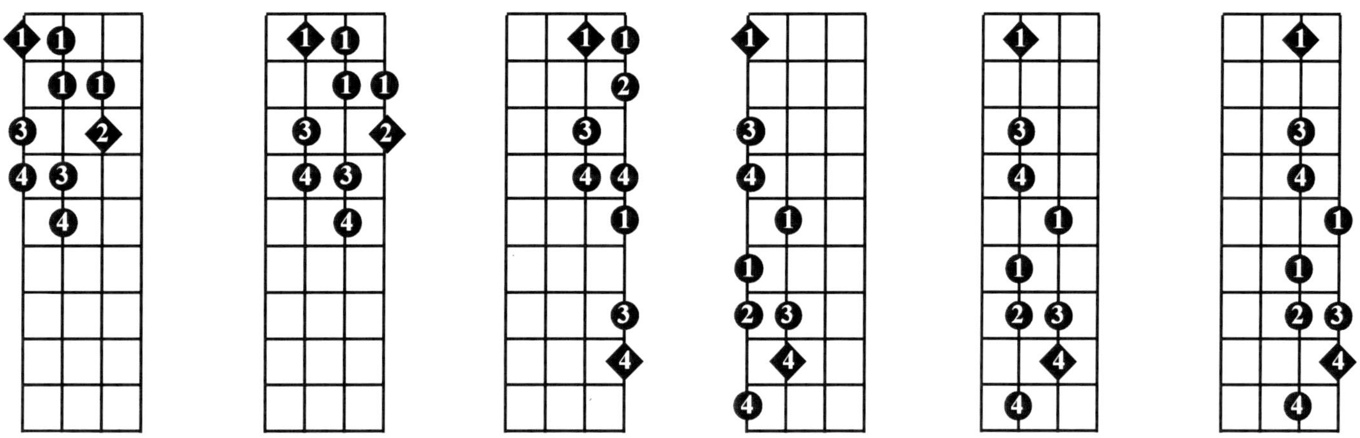

Two-Octave Patterns - Diminished (Whole-Half)

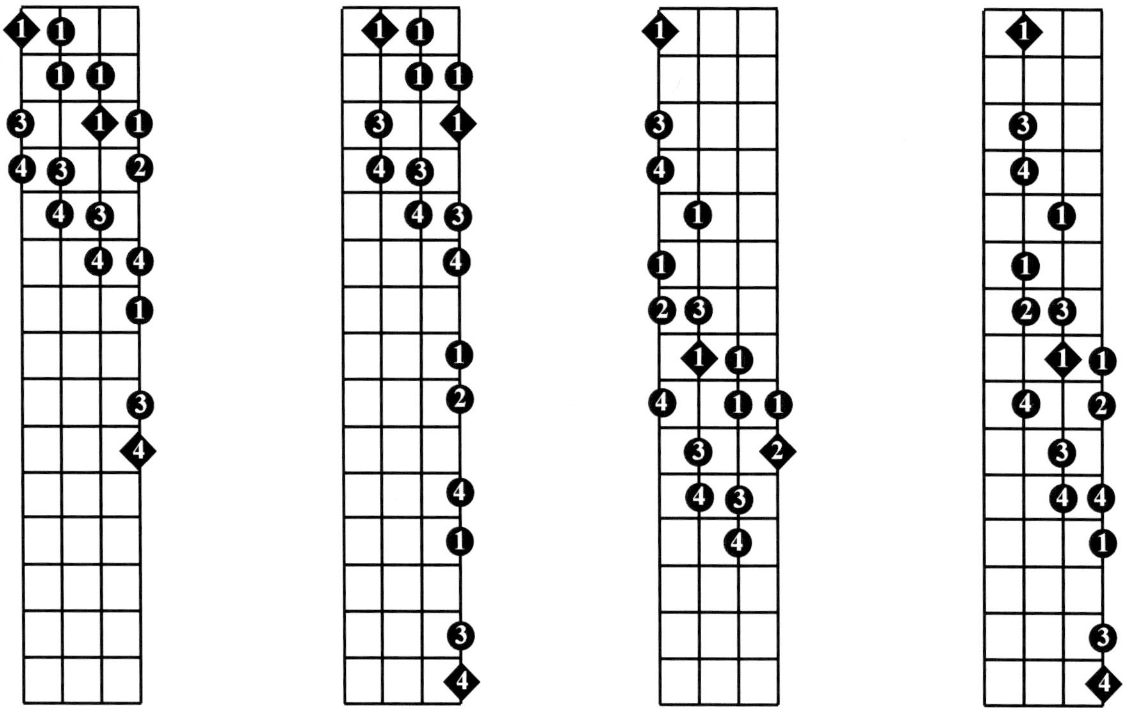

The diminished (whole-half) scale can be used to play over diminished seventh chords. The rhythm track below makes use of diminished chords in all twelve keys. Use this track to practice the diminished (whole-half) scale ascending and descending. Also, master this scale by using sequenced scalar patterns.

CD #29

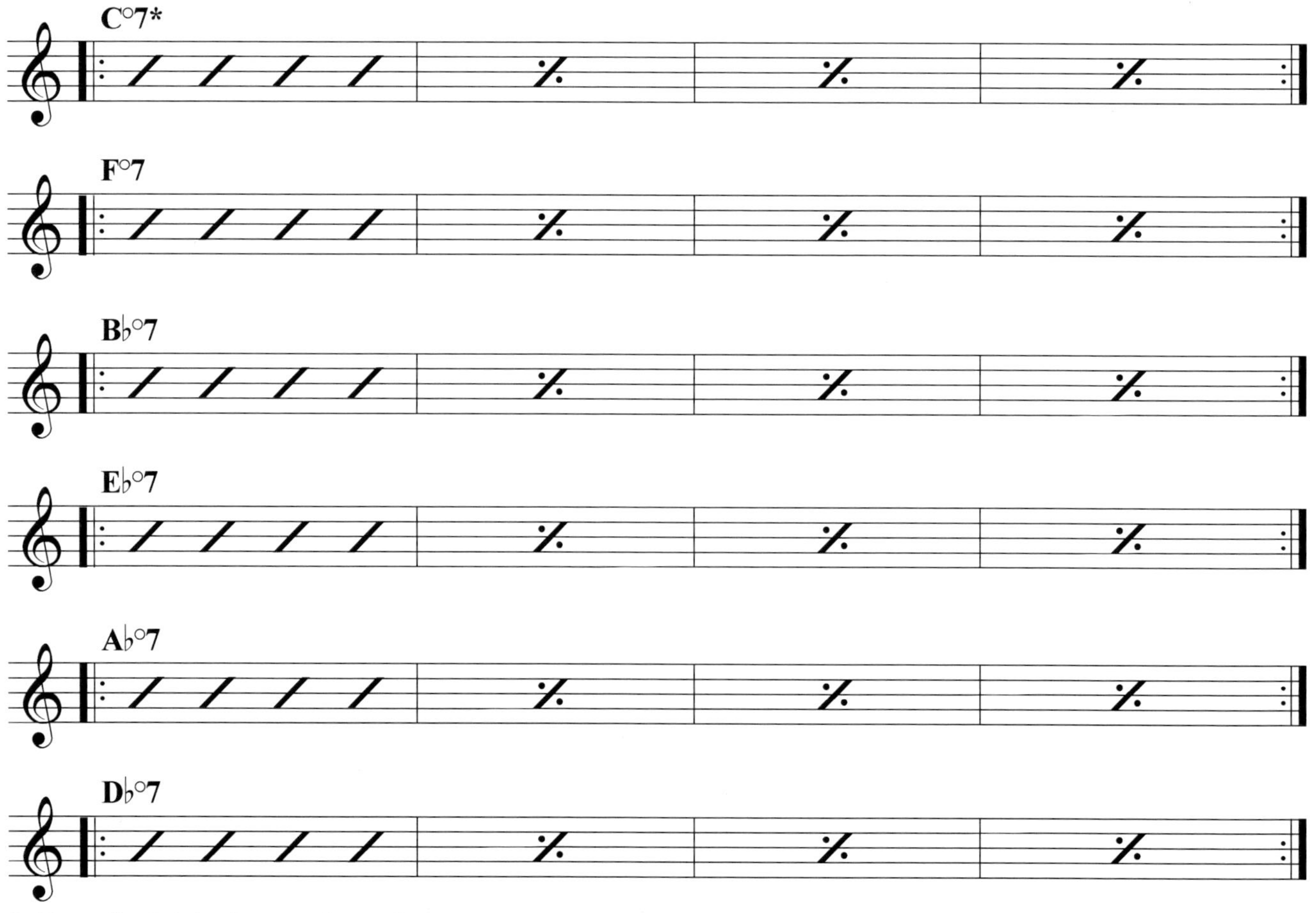

* (°7 = diminished seventh or dim7)

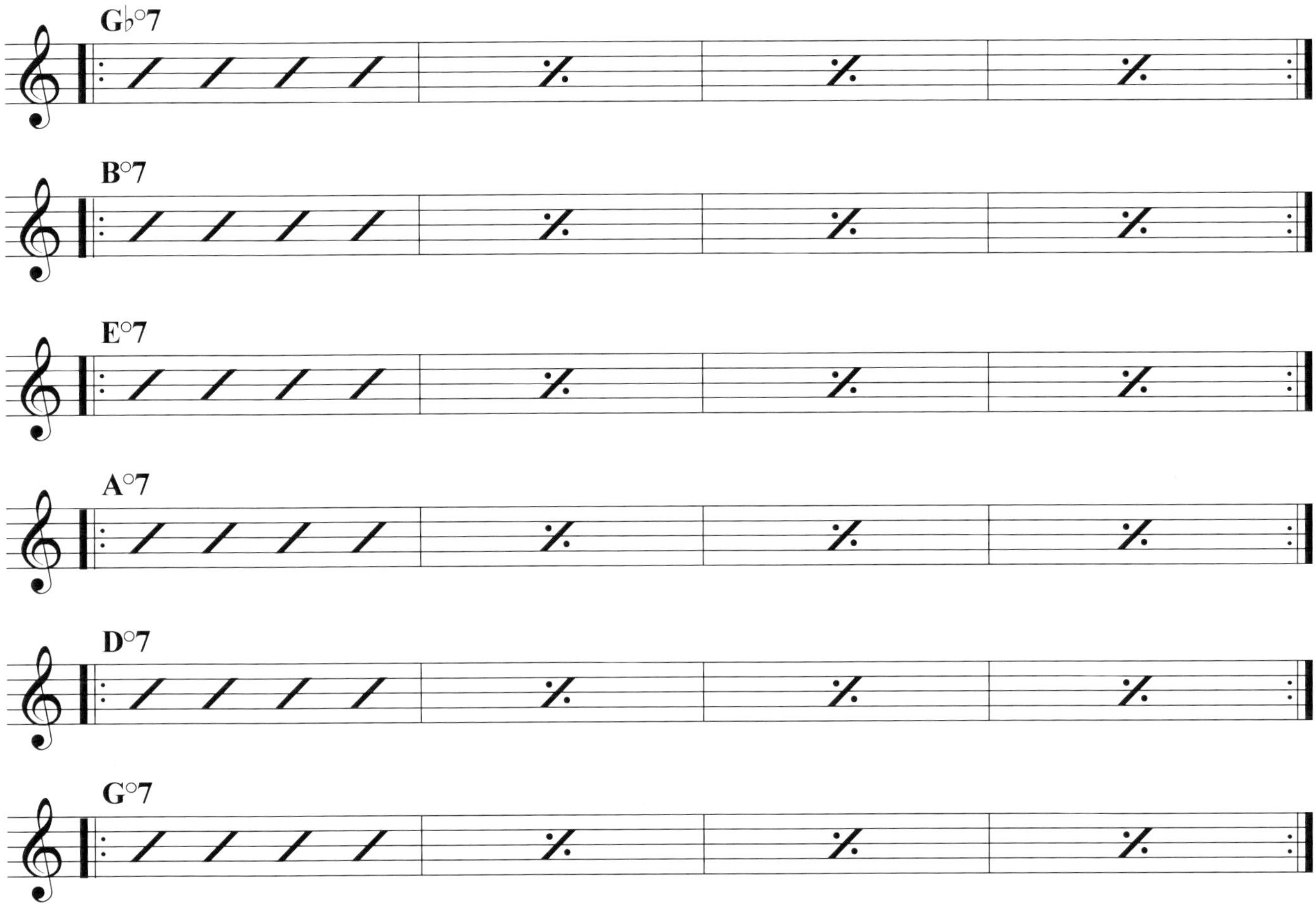

The following exercise demonstrates how the diminished (whole-half) scale can be used to improvise over diminished chords.

CD #30

Diminished Half-Whole

The diminished (half-whole) scale is shown below.

C Diminished (Half-Whole) **G Diminished (Half-Whole)**

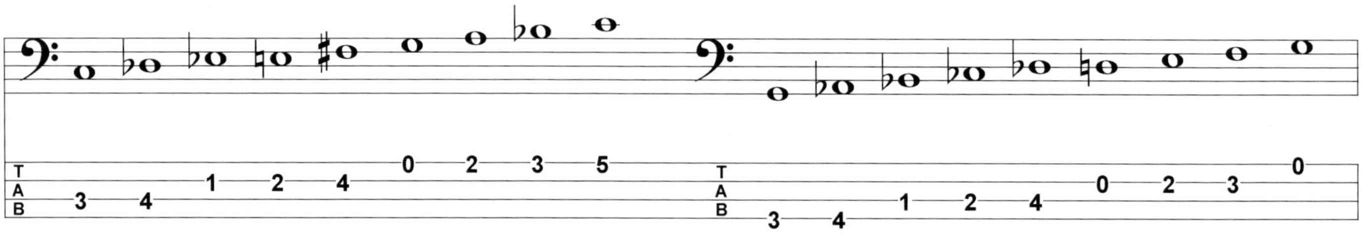

The intervallic construction and a linear diagram of this scale with the root on the fourth string are shown below. Like the diminished whole-half scale, the diminished half-whole is a symmetrical scale and is repeated every other note. The C, E♭, G♭, and A diminished half-whole scales contain the exact same notes. One-octave and two-octave patterns have also been provided.

Construction: half step, whole step, half step, whole step, half step, whole step, half step, whole step.

F Diminished (Half-Whole)

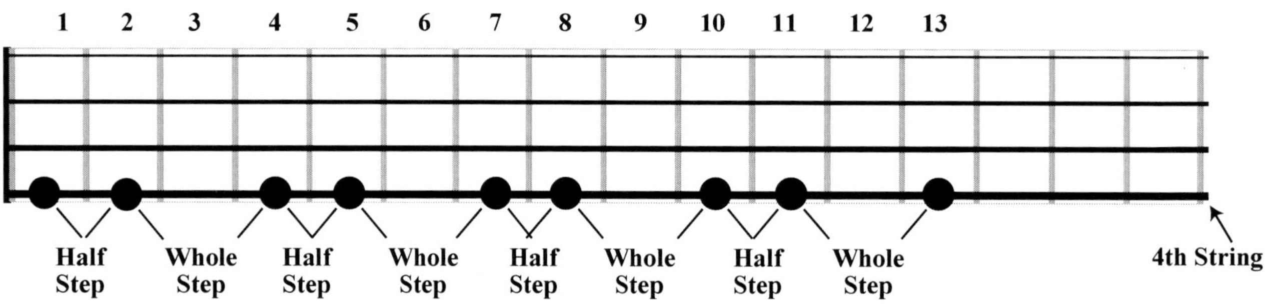

One-Octave Patterns - Diminished (Half-Whole)

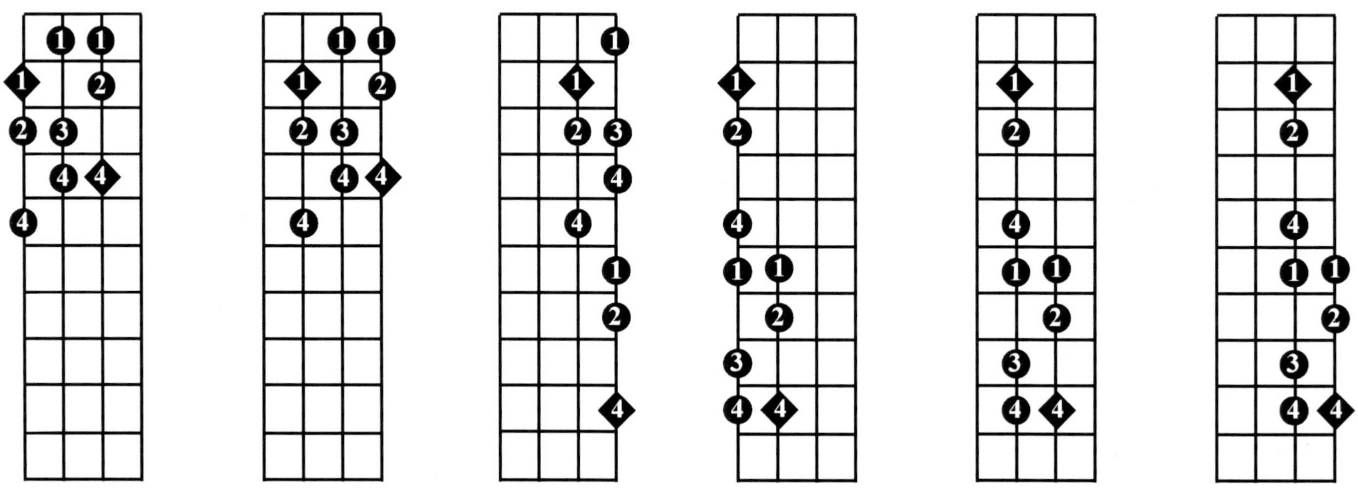

Two-Octave Patterns - Diminished (Half-Whole)

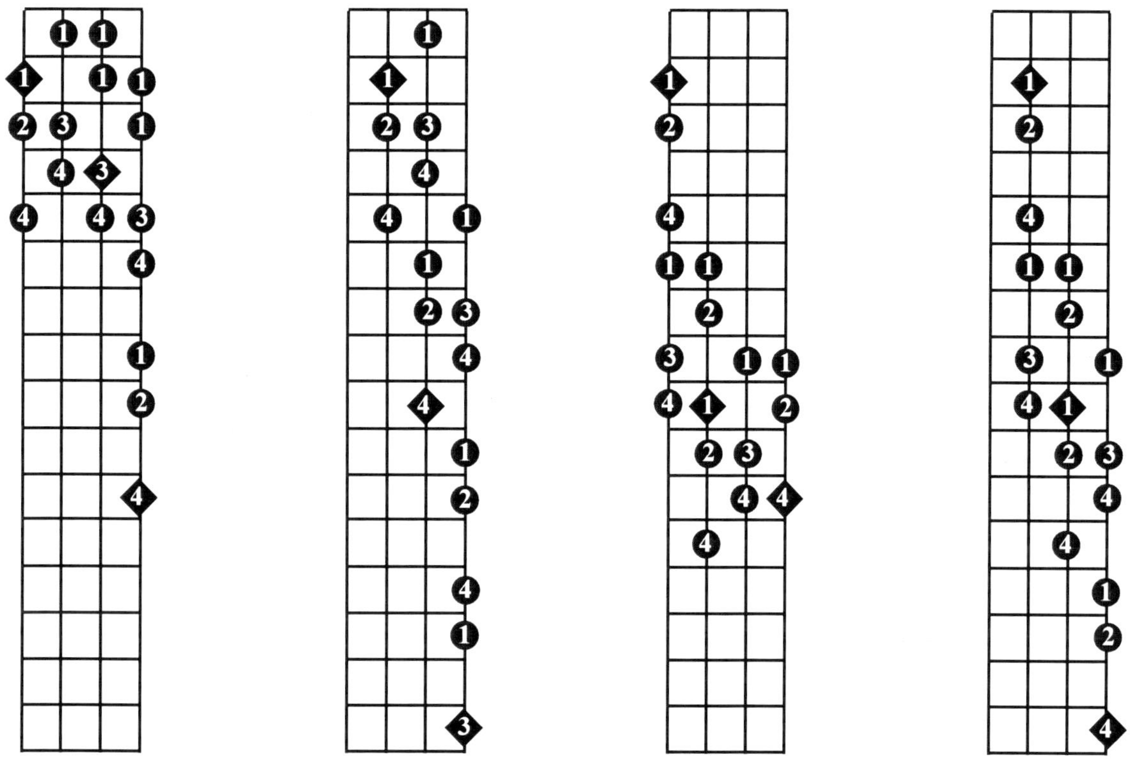

The diminished (half-whole) scale sounds nice when played against dominant seventh chords that have a flat or sharp nine (7♭9, 7♯9). The following rhythm track has been provided so that this scale may be practiced in all twelve keys against dominant seventh chords with an altered ninth. Make sure to practice the scale ascending and descending and with sequenced scalar patterns.

CD #31 (also try with #11)

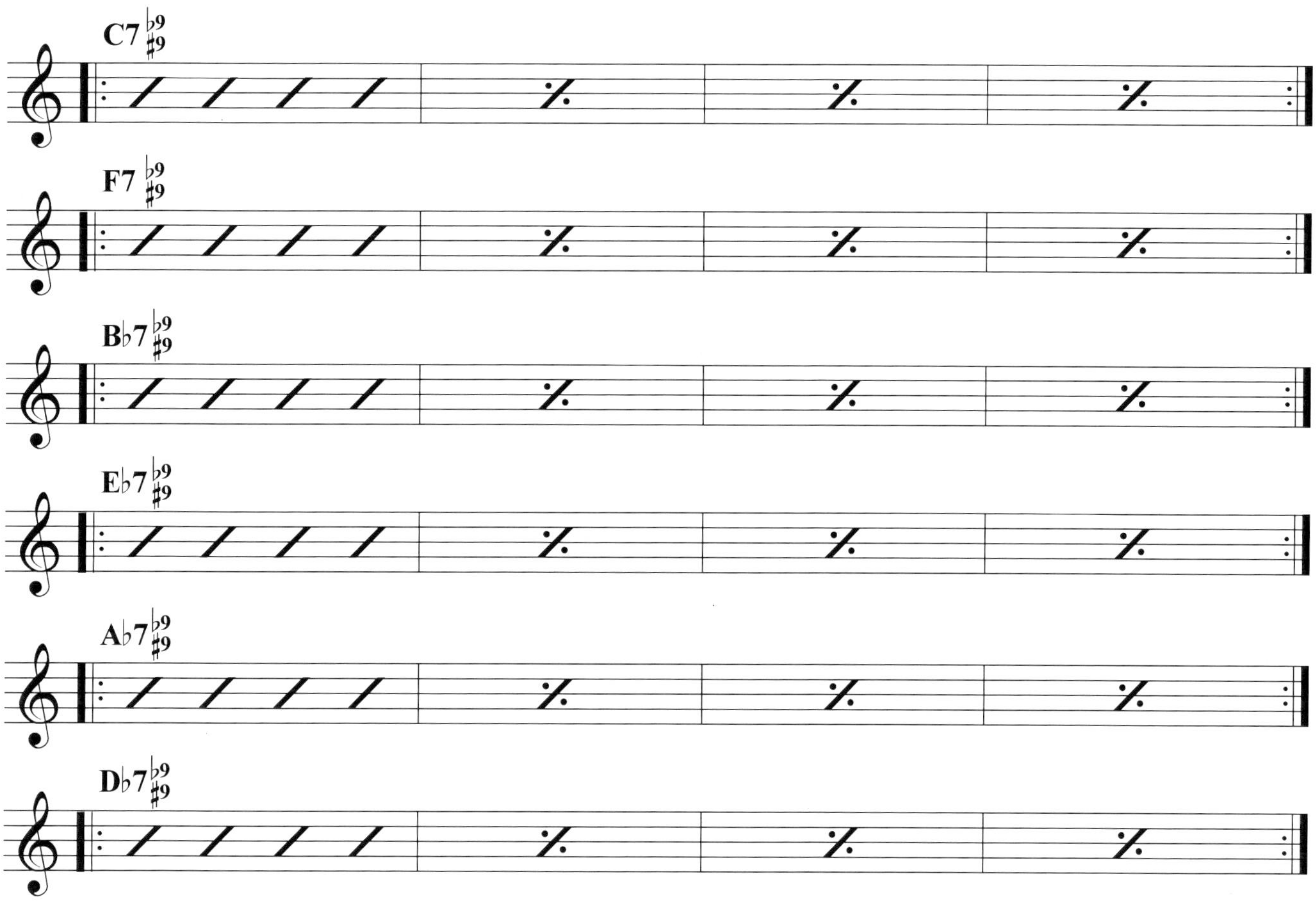

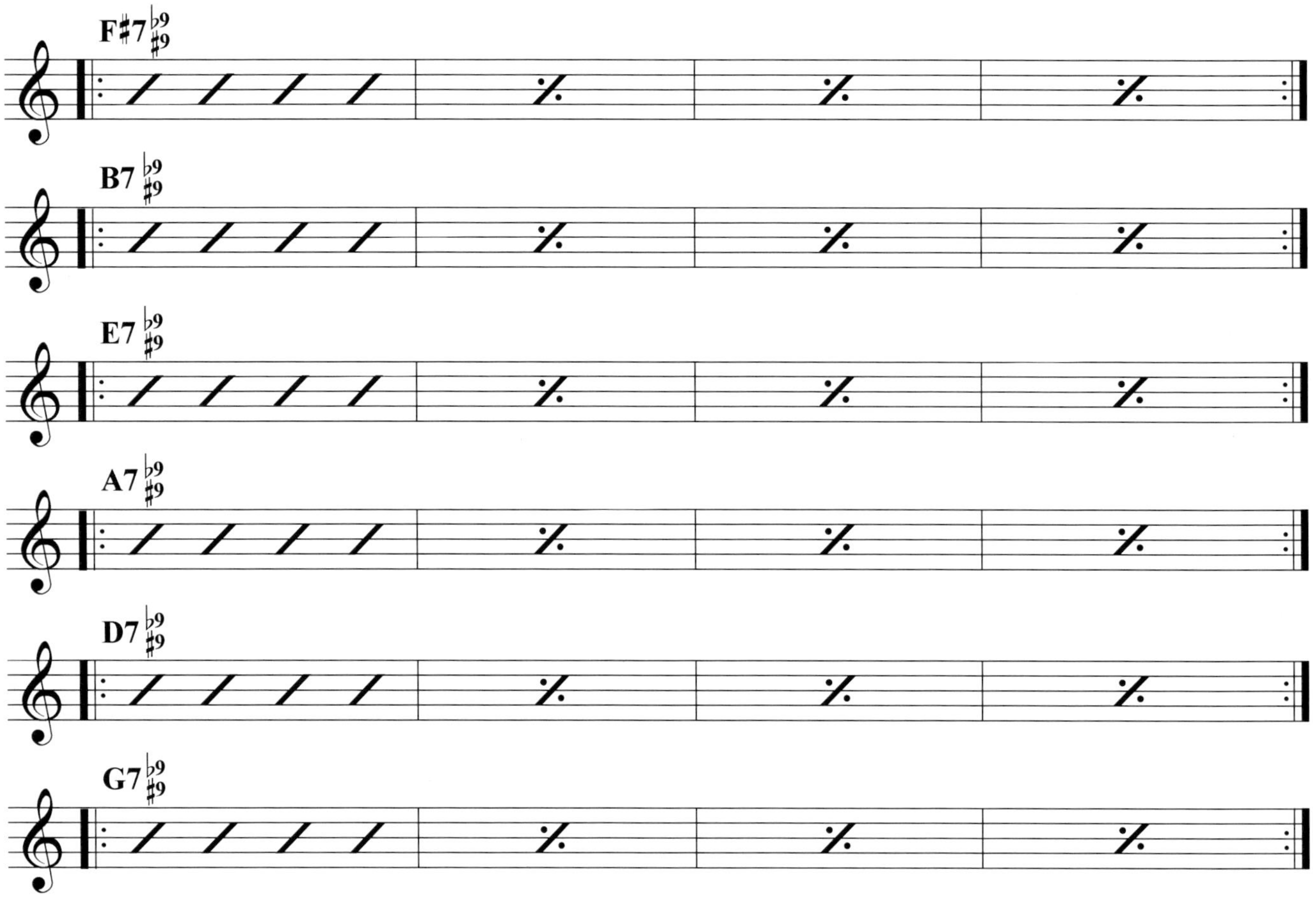

The following exercise demonstrates how the diminished (half-whole) scale may be used to improvise over the dominant seventh chords with an altered ninth.

CD #32

Whole-Tone Scale

Like the diminished scale, the whole-tone scale is a symmetrical scale. It is made up entirely of whole steps. Because of its construction, every other note can be the root of the scale. This means there are only two whole-tone scales that contain different notes. The C whole-tone scale contains the same notes as the D, E, F♯ (G♭), G♯(A♭), and A♯(B♭) whole tone scales. The C♯ whole-tone scale contains all of the other notes and roots for the other whole-tone scales. The whole-tone scale is shown below.

C Whole-Tone **C♯ Whole-Tone**

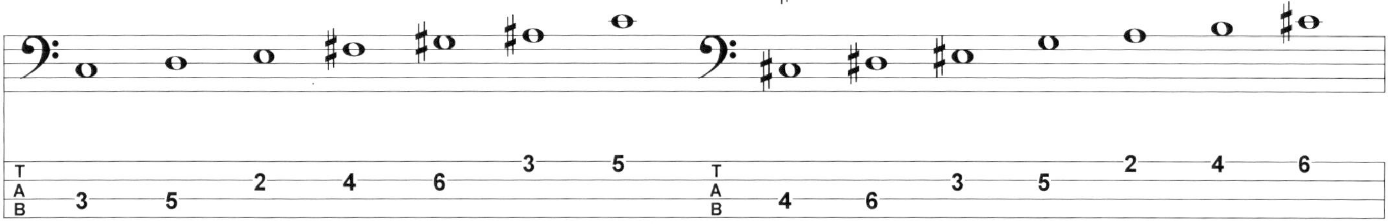

The whole-tone scale's construction and a linear diagram with the root on the fourth string are given below. One-octave and two-octave finger patterns are also given.

Construction: whole step, whole step, whole step, whole step, whole step, whole step

F Whole-Tone Scale

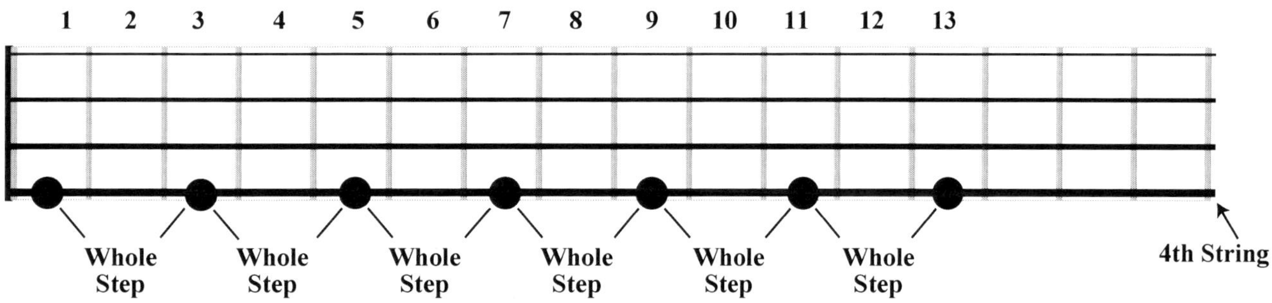

One-Octave Patterns - Whole Tone

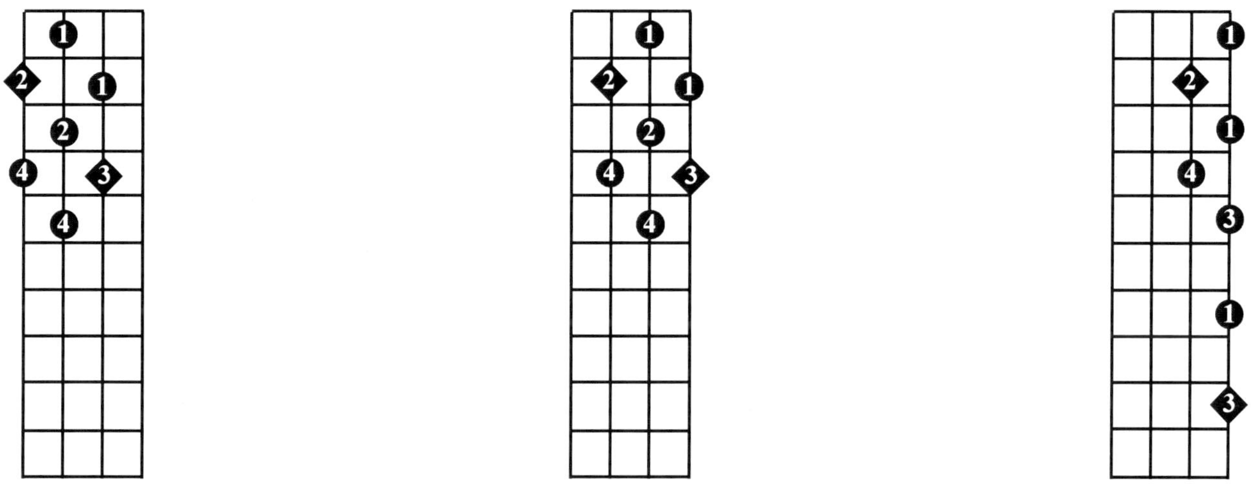

Two-Octave Patterns - Whole Tone

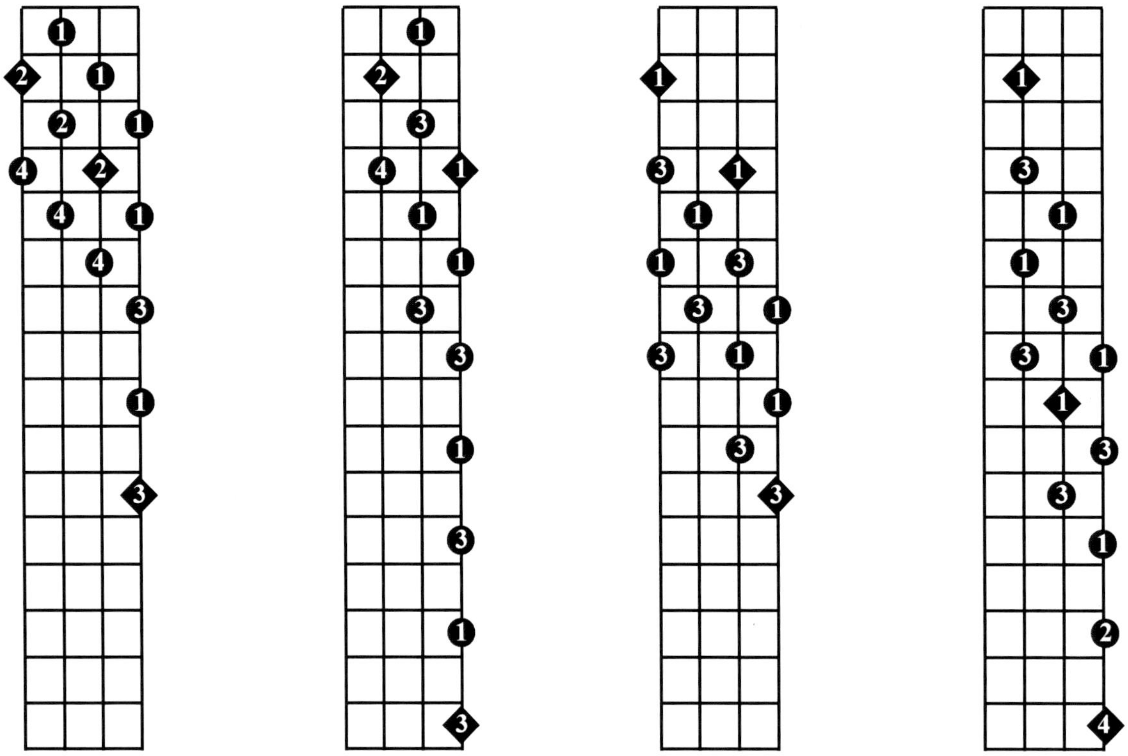

The whole-tone scale works great over augmented chords as well as dominant seventh chords with an altered fifth (♭5, ♯5). For this reason, the following rhythm track has been provided. Practice this scale ascending and descending with the following chords. Also, make use of sequenced scalar patterns when learning this scale.

CD #33 (also try with #11)

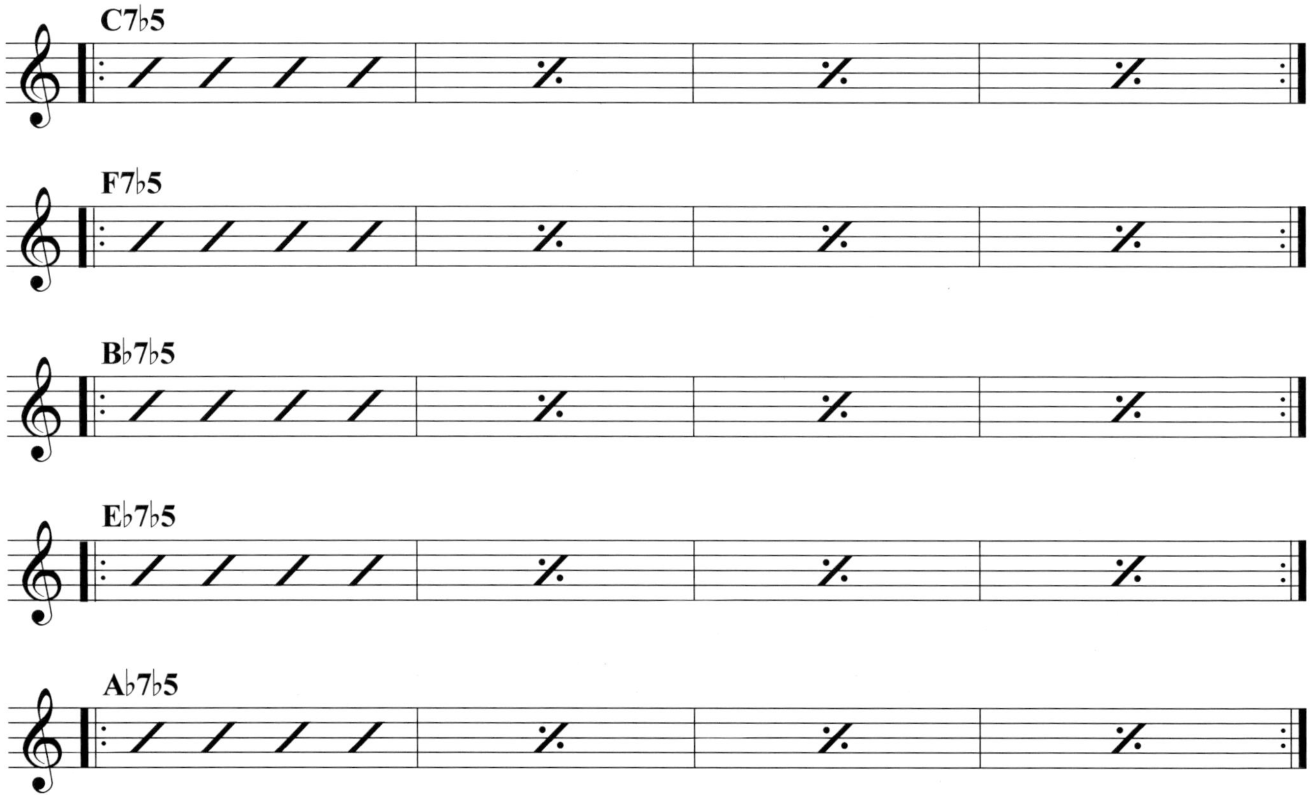

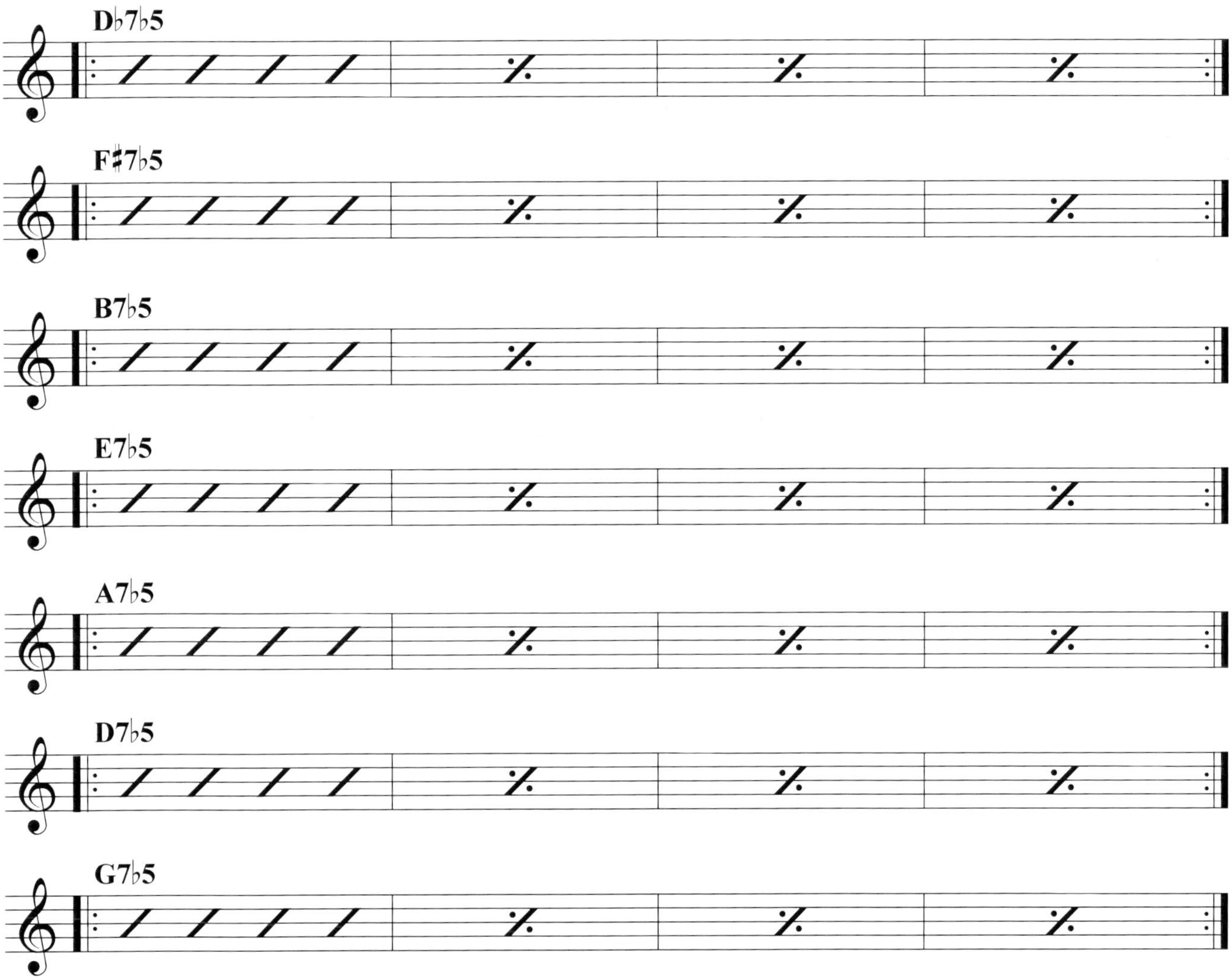

The following exercise makes use of the B♭ whole-tone scale.

CD #34

Chromatic Scale

The chromatic scale is made up entirely of half steps. It is shown below with notes being sharped as it ascends and notes being flatted as it descends.

C Chromatic Scale

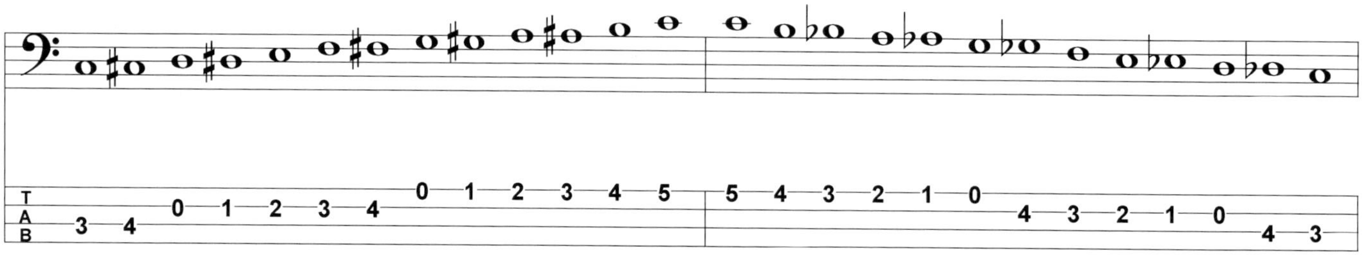

The construction and linear diagram on the fourth string for the chromatic scale are shown below. One-octave and two-octave fingering diagrams have also been provided. Because the scale is made up of half steps only and every note in the octave is utilized, every note may be the root. This scale may be used to improvise over any chord. For this reason, no rhythm track has been provided for this scale. The student should practice this scale with any of the other rhythm tracks that were used for the other scales covered in this text. Having control over this scale will bring versatility to any bassist. It may be used in fast runs or provide delicate connections from one scale to the next.

Construction: twelve half steps.

F Chromatic Scale

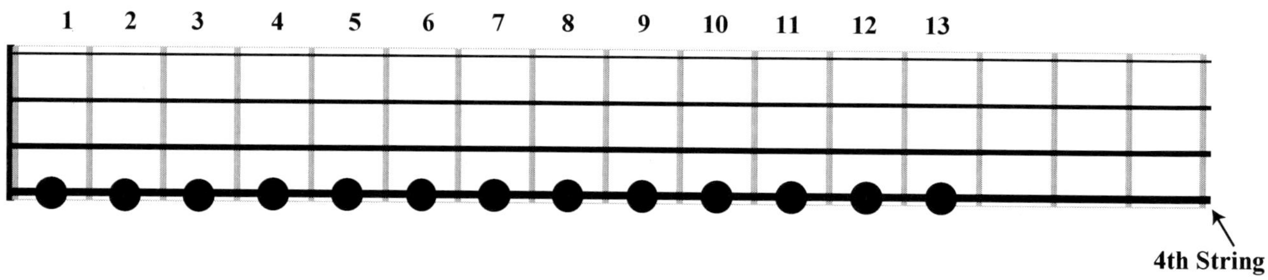

One-Octave Patterns - Chromatic

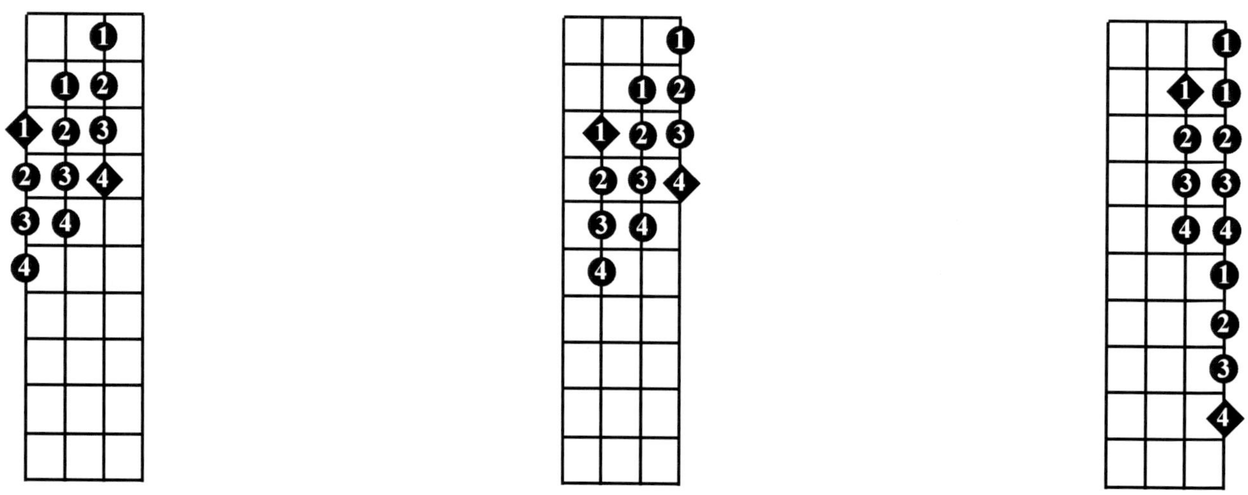

Two-Octave Patterns - Chromatic

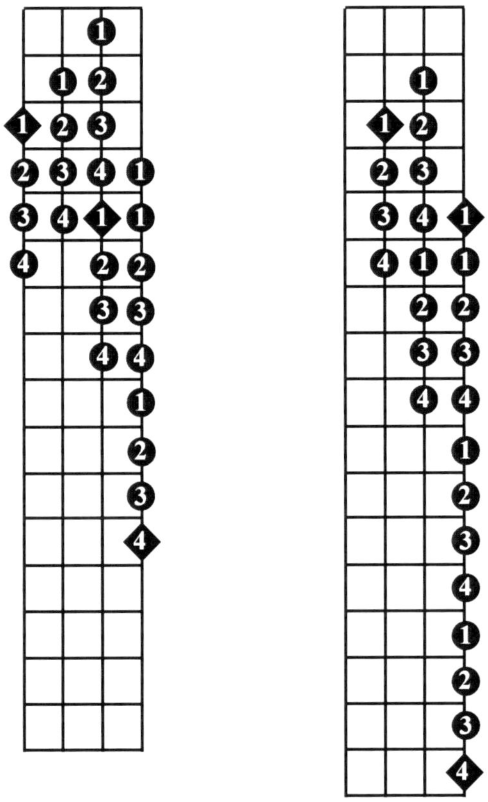

The following exercise demonstrates how the chromatic scale may be used over a seventh chord. Because every note on the bass is found in the chromatic scale, one must be careful how it used. In this example, the chromatic scale is used to lead into and out of chord tones. Notice how the chord tones are emphasized by the use of chromatic tones. The chromatic scale may be used this way against any chord. A chord construction chart has been provided on page 80 for the bassist to see the chord tones for the most common chords in jazz.

CD #35

This book has explained many of the scales and modes used in jazz improvisation. Take the information provided and now build upon it by studying the music of former and present jazz masters. Understanding the scales used in jazz allows the student to analyze great players in a methodical way. This will lead to a better understanding and knowledge of how to create sophisticated improvised solos. Good luck with the pursuance of this great American art form.

Chord Name (Chord Symbol)	Chord Tones
Major	root(note with the same letter name as the name of the chord), 3, 5
minor	root, ♭3, 5
dim	root, ♭3, ♭5
aug	root, 3, ♯5
sus	root, 4, 5
6	root, 3, 5, 6
m6	root, ♭3, 5, 6
maj7	root, 3, 5, 7
maj7♯11	root, 3, 5, 7, ♯11 (♭5)
7	root, 3, 5, ♭7
+7 (7+)	root, 3, ♯5, ♭7
7sus	root, 4, 5, ♭7
m7	root, ♭3, 5, ♭7
m7sus	root, ♭3, 4, 5, ♭7
m+7	root, ♭3, 5, 7
m7♭5 (m7-5) (ø7)	root, ♭3, ♭5, ♭7
dim7 (°7)	root, ♭3, ♭5, ♭♭7
maj9	root, 3, 5, 7, 9
maj9♯11 (maj9+11)	root, 3, 5, 7, 9, ♯11 (♭5)
9	root, 3, 5, ♭7, 9
m9	root, ♭3, 5, ♭7, 9
add9	root, 3, 5, 9
6/9	root, 3, 5, 6, 9
6/9♯11 (6/9+11)	root, 3, 5, 6, 9, ♯11 (♭5)
11	root, 3, 5, ♭7, 9, 11
13	root, 3, 5, ♭7, 9, 11, 13
7♭5 (7-5)	root, 3, ♭5, ♭7
7♯5 (7+5)	root, 3, ♯5, ♭7
7♭9 (7-9)	root, 3, 5, ♭7, ♭9
7♯9 (7+9)	root, 3, 5, ♭7, ♯9